John Davidson's guide to

Walking and Cycling in the Highlands

More routes across the north of Scotland

Published in 2014 by
Tread Wisely Publications
17 Stratherrick Gardens
Inverness, IV2 4LX
www.treadwiselypublications.com

Printed in Scotland by J Thomson Colour Printers

ISBN # 978-0-9565999-1-9

A catalogue record for this book is
available from the British Library

The author, cartographer and publisher have made every effort to ensure the information and route descriptions provided here are a true and accurate reflection. However, we cannot be held liable for your safety whilst following these routes. You must take responsibility for your own actions and undertake any of the routes knowing your own abilities and limitations.

Photographs

Opposite page: The author on the old railway line between Findochty and Cullen.

Overleaf: On the Coire Dubh Mor path en route to Beinn Eighe.

MIX
Paper from responsible sources
FSC® C023105
FSC
www.fsc.org

John Davidson's guide to

Walking and Cycling in the Highlands

More routes across the north of Scotland

TREAD WISELY PUBLICATIONS

For Clara and Jennifer

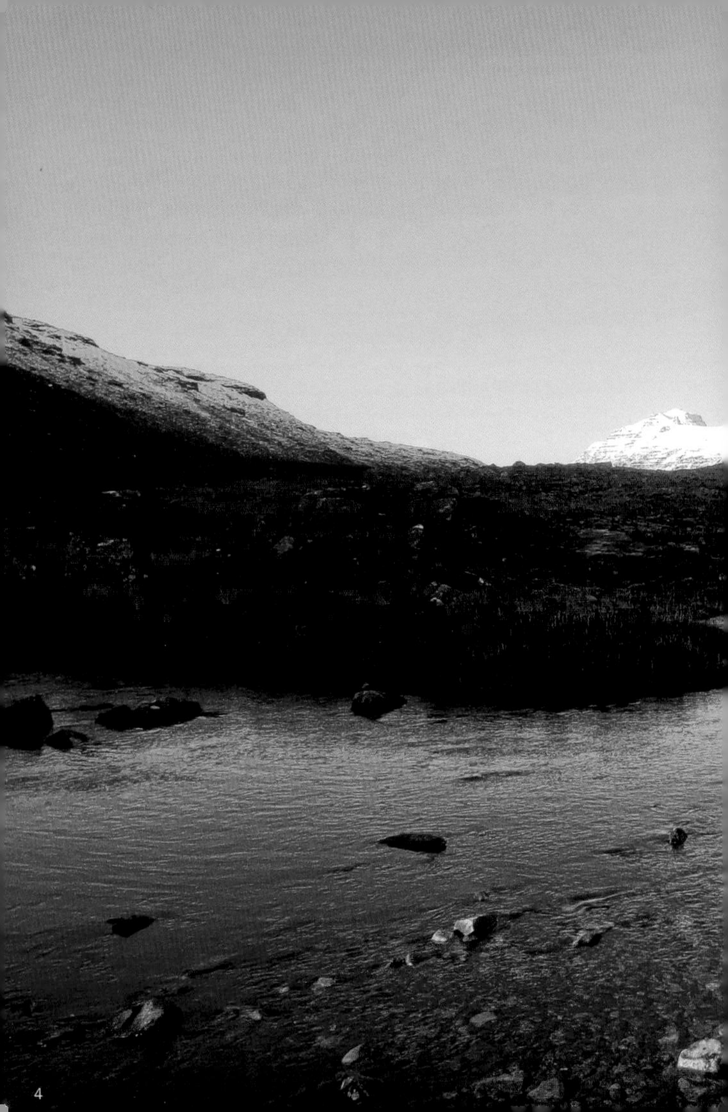

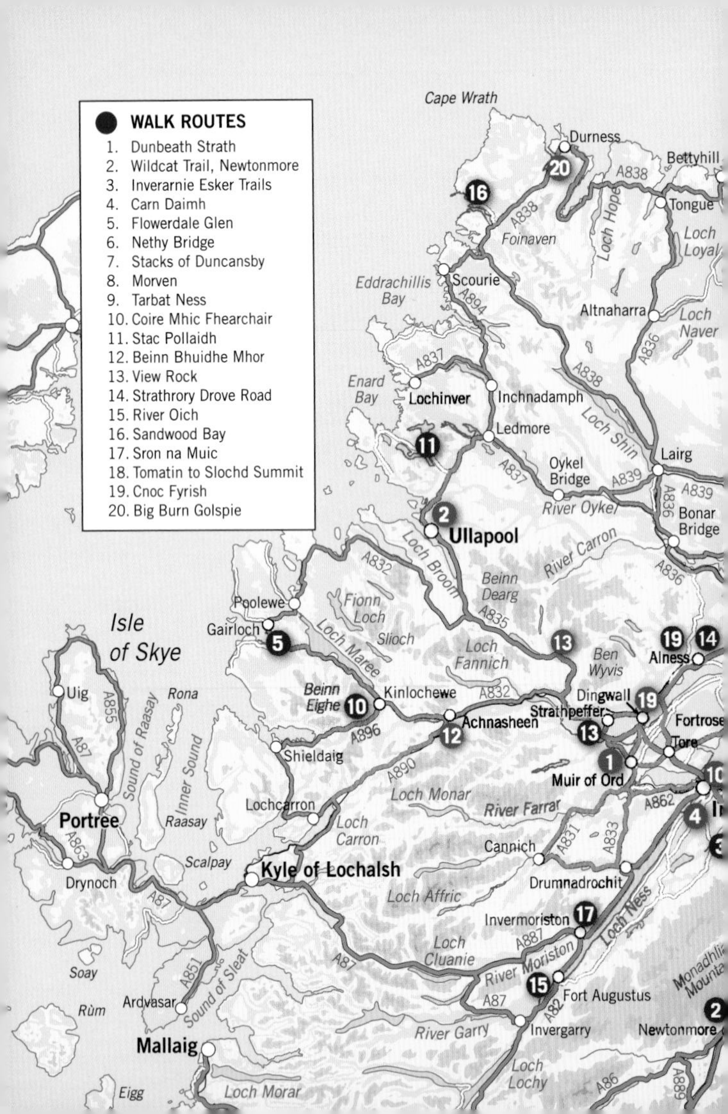
WALK ROUTES
1. Dunbeath Strath
2. Wildcat Trail, Newtonmore
3. Inverarnie Esker Trails
4. Carn Daimh
5. Flowerdale Glen
6. Nethy Bridge
7. Stacks of Duncansby
8. Morven
9. Tarbat Ness
10. Coire Mhic Fhearchair
11. Stac Pollaidh
12. Beinn Bhuidhe Mhor
13. View Rock
14. Strathrory Drove Road
15. River Oich
16. Sandwood Bay
17. Sron na Muic
18. Tomatin to Slochd Summit
19. Cnoc Fyrish
20. Big Burn Golspie
Cape Wrath
Durness
Bettyhill
A838
Tongue
Loch Hope
Foinaven
Loch Loyal
Eddrachillis Bay
Scourie
A894
Altnaharra
Loch Naver
A836
A837
Enard Bay
Lochinver
Inchnadamph
Loch Shin
Ledmore
Lairg
Oykel Bridge
A839
River Oykel
Bonar Bridge
Ullapool
Loch Broom
River Carron
A832
Beinn Dearg
A835
Poolewe
Fionn Loch
Isle of Skye
Gairloch
Loch Maree
Slioch
Loch Fannich
Ben Wyvis
Alness
Uig
A855
Rona
Beinn Eighe
Kinlochewe
Dingwall
Strathpeffer
Achnasheen
Fortrose
A87
Sound of Raasay
A896
Shieldaig
Tore
Inner Sound
A890
Muir of Ord
Loch Monar
River Farrar
A862
Portree
Lochcarron
Loch Carron
A863
Raasay
Cannich
A831
A833
Scalpay
Kyle of Lochalsh
Drumnadrochit
Drynoch
Loch Affric
Loch Ness
Invermoriston
Loch Cluanie
A887
River Moriston
Soay
A851
Sound of Sleat
Fort Augustus
Monadhliath Mountains
Rùm
Ardvasar
A82
Invergarry
River Garry
Newtonmore
Mallaig
Loch Lochy
A86
A889
Eigg
Loch Morar

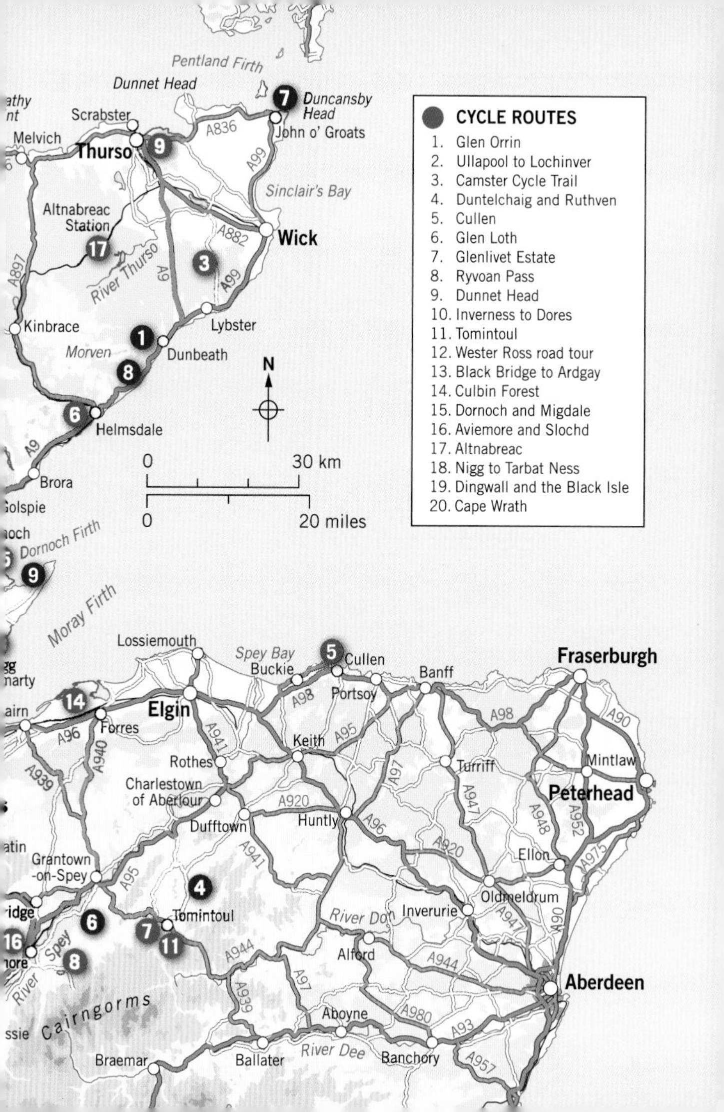
CYCLE ROUTES
1. Glen Orrin
2. Ullapool to Lochinver
3. Camster Cycle Trail
4. Duntelchaig and Ruthven
5. Cullen
6. Glen Loth
7. Glenlivet Estate
8. Ryvoan Pass
9. Dunnet Head
10. Inverness to Dores
11. Tomintoul
12. Wester Ross road tour
13. Black Bridge to Ardgay
14. Culbin Forest
15. Dornoch and Migdale
16. Aviemore and Slochd
17. Altnabreac
18. Nigg to Tarbat Ness
19. Dingwall and the Black Isle
20. Cape Wrath
N
0
30 km
0
20 miles
Pentland Firth
Dunnet Head
Duncansby Head
John o' Groats
Scrabster
Melvich
Thurso
A836
A99
Sinclair's Bay
Altnabreac Station
Wick
A882
River Thurso
A9
A897
Kinbrace
Lybster
Morven
Dunbeath
Helmsdale
Brora
Dornoch Firth
Moray Firth
Lossiemouth
Spey Bay
Buckie
Cullen
Portsoy
Banff
Fraserburgh
Elgin
Forres
A96
A98
A940
A939
A941
A95
Keith
Rothes
Charlestown of Aberlour
Dufftown
A920
Huntly
A97
Turriff
A947
A948
A952
A90
Mintlaw
Peterhead
Ellon
A975
Oldmeldrum
Inverurie
Grantown-on-Spey
Tomintoul
River Don
Alford
A944
A939
Aberdeen
Spey
River
Cairngorms
Aboyne
A980
A93
Braemar
Ballater
River Dee
Banchory
A957

Introduction

↑ Loch Ness from Dores beach (Cycle 10)

→ The Hydro bothy on the Glen Orrin ride (Cycle 1)

↓ Sign to the Stacks of Duncansby from the lighthouse (Walk 7)

The excitement of exploring a new route or rediscovering an old favourite is one of the joys of being in the outdoors. Those moments of sheer pleasure when you turn a corner and see a new view stretching out to the horizon are hard to beat.

It's my hope that there'll be something in this new walking and cycling guide that inspires you to explore and enjoy the Highlands and some of the wonderful places it has to offer.

Some of us are fortunate enough to live in this special part of the world while others travel hundreds and even thousands of miles to visit. We can all share in the beauty and the opportunities these landscapes provide – from twisting footpaths to roads and trails for exhilarating cycling, it can all be found here in the Highlands. Sometimes it's closer than you think.

So take a look through these pages and be inspired to get out – whether on foot or two wheels – and experience this spectacular area at your own pace.

Many of these routes have featured in my Active Outdoors column, which appears in a number of newspapers across the Highlands and Moray, while I have chosen some purely for inclusion

in this guidebook. Some are favourites that I never get tired of, some are one-off excursions that made excellent outings – but they have all made me come home smiling!

I hope they have the same effect on you, and you continue to enjoy them for many years to come.

Being prepared

It's important to be prepared for any of the routes in this guide. The weather in the Highlands can be unpredictable, so even on the more straightforward routes you should take waterproofs and wear decent footwear.

On the more remote and technical routes it will be necessary to consider the weather conditions before deciding to undertake the trip. Check the weather forecasts – for mountain areas visit www.mwis.org.uk for daily updates to conditions.

In winter a few of the higher graded routes become very technical indeed and you should be certain that you have the necessary skills and equipment before undertaking them in these conditions. Remember, on higher ground it can even snow in the middle of summer sometimes!

Many of the routes enter areas with limited or zero mobile phone coverage, so you must be able to be self-sufficient.

The most important thing at any time is to be ready for anything, so I suggest carrying sufficient clothing to keep you warm and dry for the duration and take enough food and drink to help maintain energy levels and hydration throughout the walk or ride. You should also carry emergency items such as a first-aid kit.

I have intentionally not given expected times for the routes, because that can vary enormously depending on age, experience and personal fitness levels. This guide allows you to plan your trip around the details given so you can have an enjoyable and rewarding experience.

Access

The Land Reform Act (2003) in conjunction with the Scottish Outdoor Access Code states that you have the right to be on most land for recreational activities such as walking and cycling.

This right comes with responsibilities, including respecting people's privacy and their livelihoods, as well as the environment. For more details visit the website below.

How to use this guide

The routes in this book vary from gentle excursions near towns and villages to big adventures through remote countryside. They have been described as honestly and accurately as possible, allowing the reader to plan an outing using the text and accompanying sketch map.

It is highly recommended that walkers and riders take the suggested map with them when going on any of the routes in the guide – and know how to use it along with a compass, particularly for the more difficult ones.

After a short summary, each route begins with the following information:

Grade ❶ Straightforward routes that are either suitable for families or that don't need much navigation **❷** Routes that require some skills, particularly navigation **❸** Routes where navigation skills are required; these routes may enter very rough or remote areas with no facilities for many miles and may need specialist skills or equipment, particularly in winter
Distance Total distances are given in miles and kilometres
Start/finish Point of start and finish of the route
Surface Brief summary of what types of surface or terrain you can expect on the route
Map A suggested map or maps which should be taken

Map Key

▬▬▬	A road	**Start**	Route starting point
═══	B road	◄──	Route direction
═══	Minor road	● ● ●	Cycle route
┄┄┄	Track	○ ○ ○	Walk route
╌ ╌ ╌	Path	**1** **7**	National Cycle Network
──●──	Rail	**P**	Parking
▨	Woodland	⌂	Picnic site
·706	Heights in metres	▢	Cafe
	910m (3000ft) approx	⚒	Bike repairs
	610m (2000ft) approx	⛊	Campsite
	305m (1000ft)	▲	Youth hostel
	183m (600ft)	⚏	Toilets
	0		

↗ Loch a' Chroisg near Achnasheen (Cycle 12)

All maps: © www.helenstirlingmaps.com 2014. Contains Ordnance Survey Data.
© Crown Copyright and Database Right 2012

WALK 1

Take a step back in time on a trek through a lonely strath

Grade 2/3 Navigation skills required on full route
Distance 3.5 miles / 5.5 km shorter circular route; 7.5 miles / 12 km total for the full route
Start/finish Dunbeath Old Mill
Surface Riverside path, vehicle track, minor road, pathless boggy hillside
Map OS Landranger 17

Life in this remote strath must have been very different in days gone by. Exploring alongside the beautiful Dunbeath Water, this walk visits a number of historic sites, each with its own story to tell – or to keep secret.

There are two options – a shorter circular walk or the full route to the chambered cairn on Cnoc na Maranaich. Whichever you choose, it's a spectacular place to visit and offers wonderful walking. Car parking is available behind the old Meal Mill just north of the Thomas Telford bridge.

An information panel at the start of the walk shows you some of the highlights ahead on this fantastic outing. Follow the narrow path alongside the river and you'll soon reach the first historic point of interest. Chapel Hill is believed to be the site of an ancient monastery with its large walls, the ruins of which are visible to the right from the path.

Over the suspension bridge across the Houstry Burn you can detour to one of the best preserved brochs in Caithness by heading through the gate and along the obvious path.

Back on the route, the trail continues along the river, passing a rickety bridge before going through woodland. At one point the path rises away from the river before dropping down to another, more sturdy bridge. This is where the shorter walk heads back, crossing the river to pick up the return route as described below.

Ahead lies an impressive gorge known as the Prisoner's Leap, across which Ian McMormack Gunn is said to have leapt to his freedom having been imprisoned in nearby Forse Castle by the Keiths. To judge for yourself, continue past the bridge then follow a clear path up to the right before you reach the rocky gorge.

At a fence, go right and follow it up to a vehicle track. Turn left to go deeper into the strath past ruined farmhouses at Loedebest and on to the white-walled Tutnaguail Cemetery.

From the burial ground, take a bearing across the rough moorland to the summit of Cnoc na Maranaich, watching out for boggy rivers and tussocky ground. The hill steepens as you approach the summit, marked by a standing stone.

Head south-east across the empty moors – picking up a very old track if you are lucky enough to locate it – to Carn Liath, the remains of a long chambered burial cairn, then cut back to the track at Loedebest.

Return past the Prisoner's Leap to the bridge and cross it to follow a wonderful path up between the trees, keeping left at a fork. Go left onto a minor road ahead then take the first road left after crossing the Black Water.

Follow this down to the end and go through a gate to continue on a rough farm track which leads to a grassy area beside a ruined building – once the local inn.

Cut across the field to the rickety bridge and cross it, if you dare – a previous bridge was washed away in floods and a sign warns that you cross at your own risk. Turn right the other side to follow the path back to the old mill at the start of this unique heritage trail.

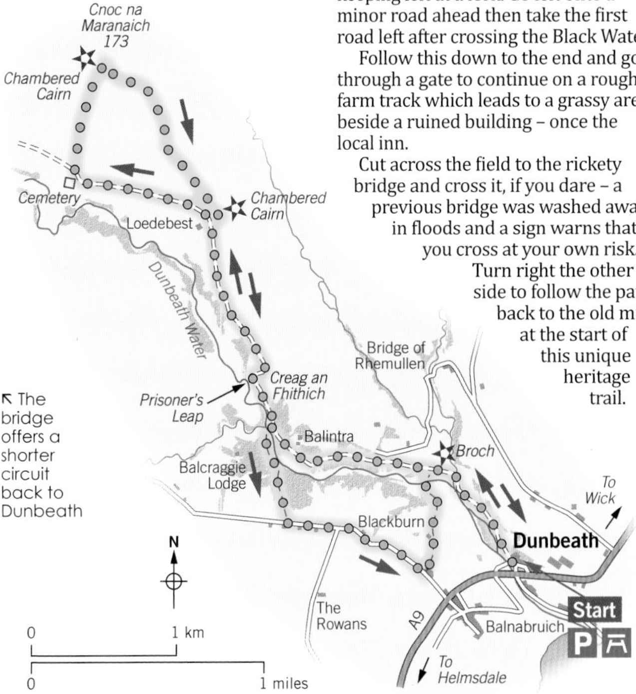

↖ The bridge offers a shorter circuit back to Dunbeath

WALK 2

Take a walk on the wild side on a fine circuit of this Badenoch village

Grade ❷ Waymarked route with some steep and rough sections
Distance 7 miles / 11 km
Start/finish Newtonmore railway station
Surface Paths and tracks, boggy in places, some steep sections, many gates and stiles; livestock on some sections
Map OS Explorer 402

The "Highland tiger" is an elusive and threatened species that nevertheless has a stronghold in parts of Badenoch and Strathspey. You're guaranteed to see a number of these wildcats on this trail around Newtonmore – albeit in the form of painted models.

You can pick the trail up at many points along the way but this route starts at the railway station, making it easy as a day trip from anywhere along the Inverness to Glasgow line.

Heading out of the station, follow the road past a few houses then turn left down a track where you see the wooden signpost directing you. Keep left in front of the memorial woodland and carefully cross the railway at the level crossing.

Hop over the stile to follow a line of trees then the edge of a field to meet the River Spey, turning right to tackle the circuit in a clockwise direction.

Follow the edge of the river, inside the fenced area at first, and then pass under the railway bridge and, beyond the campsite, the road bridge.

Past here, you follow the River Calder, a tributary of the Spey, upstream – enjoying views to the

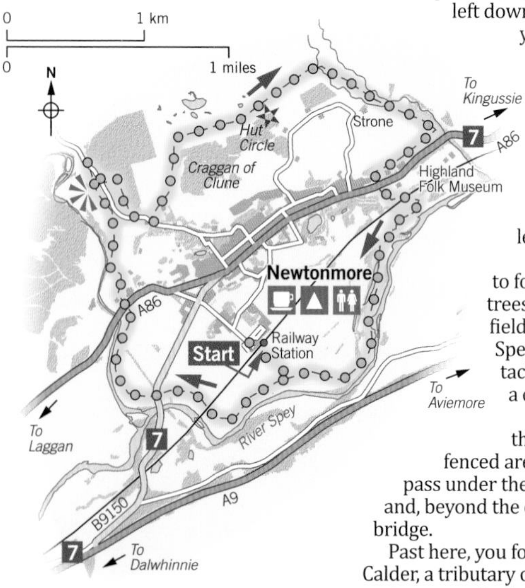

prominent ridge of Creag Dubh across the water.

Cross the A86 at Calder Bridge, going immediately left the other side of the road to follow a good path that returns to the riverside and steeply up behind a cemetery.

The sound of tumbling waterfalls accompanies you along this beautiful stretch, and you can detour down to get a closer look – but only if you're comfortable on very steep, uneven terrain.

Just before reaching the Glen Road, a viewpoint overlooking Glen Banchor offers a perfect opportunity for a rest to take in the spectacular panorama.

Take a right turn along the road until the signs point left into the woodland. Look out for a right turn in the woods before you emerge to views over the village towards the Cairngorm mountains and soon rejoin the road, where you turn left to continue.

After the cattle grid, turn left up a track which you follow to the edge of birch woods, with open views to your left to the Munro of A' Chailleach with its impressive east-facing cliffs.

Pass a cairn in the woods then continue as the track turns to a boggy path before you reach the remains of an old hut circle. Further on, cross a burn by a wooden footbridge before turning right across the grass to overlook the old crofting township of Strone.

The route then crosses another footbridge beside a lovely waterfall before following the Allt Laraidh down to meet the main road just outside the village.

Turn right at the bottom and stay on that side of the road along the trail until you are beyond the Highland Folk Museum.

A sign hidden in the hedge on the opposite side of the road points left down a tarmac track immediately before a white house.

Follow this straight on then over the railway, after which it narrows to become a nice little path that runs alongside the golf course as it meets the River Spey again. Continue over stepping stones here and there until you reach the far end of the course, where you turn right to return to the railway station.

To go to the village centre – where there is a Wildcat Trail centre run by volunteers – turn left up Station Road then right at the main road, or simply turn right to return to the station.

Creag Dubh from the Wildcat Trail above Newtonmore

Explore a remarkable landscape shaped by ice and water

Grade 1 Signed route with boggy, uneven and steep stretches
Distance 3 miles / 5 km
Start/finish Signed parking area at forest gate on B851 near Inverarnie
Surface Paths, boggy in places, some steps and steep slopes
Map Forests of Inverness leaflet (Forestry Commission)

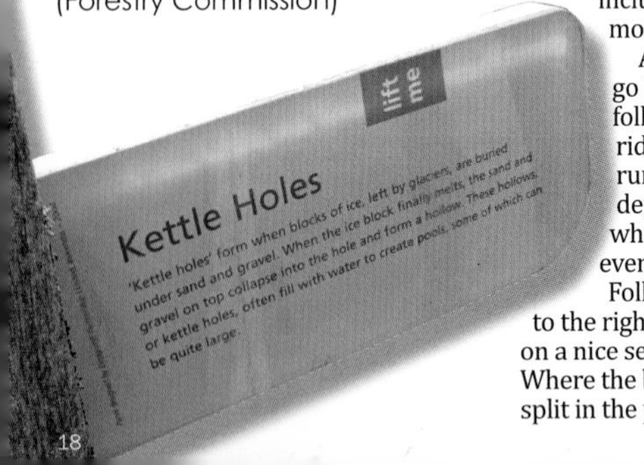

lift me
Kettle Holes
'Kettle holes' form when blocks of ice, left by glaciers, are buried under sand and gravel. When the ice block finally melts, the sand and gravel on top collapse into the hole and form a hollow. These hollows, or kettle holes, often fill with water to create pools, some of which can be quite large.

A short distance from Inverness, the Forestry Commission trails at Littlemill Woods provide a great escape as you are transported back to the ice age.

A series of "esker" ridges and "kettle hole" lochans make this a wonderful site, with twisting paths that climb and drop as they wind their way around the water and between the trees.

There are three colour-coded loops suggested on the notice board a short distance up the track from the parking area. This walk takes in a circuit including all three to make the most of a visit here.

After a short, steep hill, go left on the blue route to follow the top of an esker ridge – formed by rivers running underneath a glacier depositing sand and gravel which was exposed as the ice eventually melted.

Follow the blue markers round to the right before a quarry and head on a nice section through pine trees. Where the blue route goes right at a split in the path, turn left and join the

← The larger of the kettle hole lochans at Littlemill

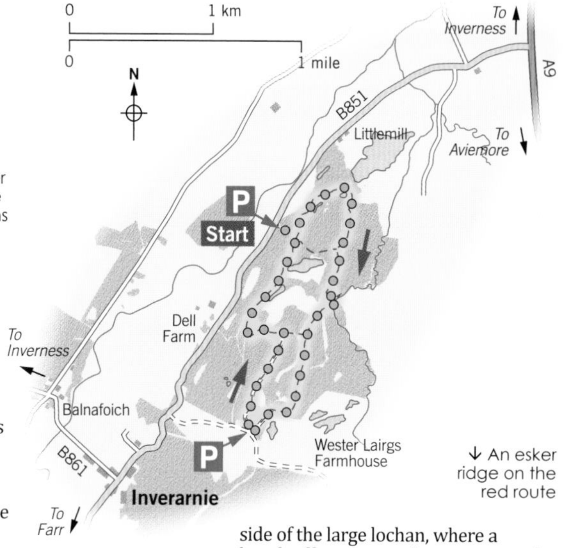

red route which soon climbs steps to offer a superb view of the largest of the lochans.

Cross a boggy area then climb a faded section of path to reach a clear track on top of another esker ridge as it cuts back right to follow the ridge.

Stay on the ridge where it becomes part of the yellow route as the red route departs to the right. At the end, drop off the ridge to the right then follow a grass path left, away from the trees, to emerge on a vehicle track.

Follow the main track right and continue to a gate at another parking area. Turn right and follow this track past a number of glacial erratics – large boulders dumped by receding glaciers.

At a turning point, go left as you rejoin the red route which meanders about until it follows another ridge that takes you along to the other side of the large lochan, where a bench offers a great place to stop and enjoy views over the surrounding countryside.

A short climb here is the last of the effort as the route continues to meet the track, where a left turn heads back down to reach the start point.

↓ An esker ridge on the red route

WALK 4

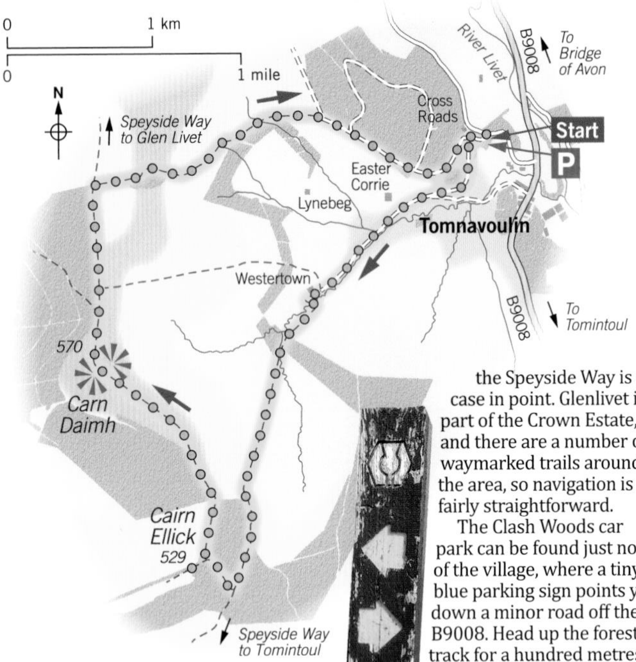

→ A wonderful path leads beside the forest

Easy hill climb is jewel in the crown on royal estate

Grade ❷ Waymarked route rising to 570m
Distance 6.5 miles / 10.5 km
Start/finish Clash Woods car park, Tomnavoulin
Surface Farm, forest and hillside tracks and paths
Map OS Explorer 419

Smaller hills can often be just as rewarding as the high mountains and this climb to the highest point on the Speyside Way is a case in point. Glenlivet is part of the Crown Estate, and there are a number of waymarked trails around the area, so navigation is fairly straightforward.

The Clash Woods car park can be found just north of the village, where a tiny blue parking sign points you down a minor road off the B9008. Head up the forest track for a hundred metres or so before going left on a wonderfully twisting path that leads along the edge of the woodland to reach a gate and stile at Eastertown.

Cross the two stiles marked with blue arrows and take the left of two farm tracks at a fork. Soon the track passes Westertown farm, where it crosses a small boardwalk beside a ford then climbs by S-bends to a gate. Continue

through a small patch of woodland and drop to cross another burn.

The path ahead goes through farmland, keeping between two fences, as it climbs to meet the corner of a forest plantation. Go through a gate into the forestry and follow the track to a junction marked by a wooden signpost.

Turn right to follow the Speyside Way towards Ballindalloch up an initially steep track. It eases after a right-hand bend, where you can to take a short detour to the top of Cairn Ellick, following a grassy track left. The cairn marking this lower top is through an opening in the trees to the left.

Returning to the main track, continue downhill to the edge of the forest. Passing over a stile, the route now joins a rocky hill track as it climbs the final rise to Carn Daimh.

A panoramic view awaits, with the Cairngorms one way and Ben Rinnes the other. It's even possible to see Morven in the far north from here.

The descent takes a path to the right of the fence along the outside of the forest plantation, very boggy in places as it passes a short-cut back to Westertown (signed Tomnavoulin) and continues to a fence, where you turn right.

Leave the Speyside Way here and continue up the incline through the heather, staying this side of the fence. Near the top the path becomes clearer and it goes left beside a lone tree before skirting round to the right and following another fence downhill.

Cross it at a stile and follow the well-used way across the field towards the gap in the trees below. The route follows the outside of the plantation around the corner then the remains of a track to enter the forest by a stile.

Keep to the forest track all the way now as it descends, quite steeply in places, along the edge of Clash Woods, with some fantastic views across the open countryside to enjoy before returning to the car park.

WALK 5

A scenic west coast circuit to reach a fine waterfall

Grade 1/2 Some route finding required on return
Distance 3.5 miles / 5.5 km
Start/finish Car park opposite harbour at Charlestown, Gairloch, Wester Ross
Surface Good waymarked paths, bumpy and rocky in places, eroded and steep near waterfall, boggy towards end
Map OS Explorer 434

A waterfall at the end of the Flowerdale Glen is easily reached on good paths, while a twisty return route offers a bit more adventure for those happy to explore further.

Cross the main road from the harbour at Charlestown, south of Gairloch, and pass an old stone bridge that leads to the inn on your right. Immediately past the bridge a sign marked "Flowerdale Waterfall Footpath" points right.

The route follows a delightful well-made path, passing a pond and a number of impressive old trees. Keep straight on at a wooden sign beside the wall, following the red waterfall route rather than the green circular.

Soon after the path bends right down a tree-lined avenue, a small red marker indicates a left turn.

Cross a bridge and keep to the path as it twists and turns to follow the Abhainn Ghlas upstream higher into the glen. Where it emerges at a track, go left to cross the burn then immediately right to follow the burn more closely on a nice path.

This meets a track from Flowerdale Mains and you continue right as the red marker confirms. As the track gets higher, ignore any turn-offs and go straight ahead, occasionally catching a glimpse of the waterfall further on.

The way ahead rises gently to reach a large wooden bridge. There's a beautiful view of the falls from here but the path up to them is eroded and very steep in places, passing under boughs of trees which mean you have to duck and cover here and there!

At the top there's a lovely view west over Loch Gairloch and out into the Atlantic past Longa Island. Continuing

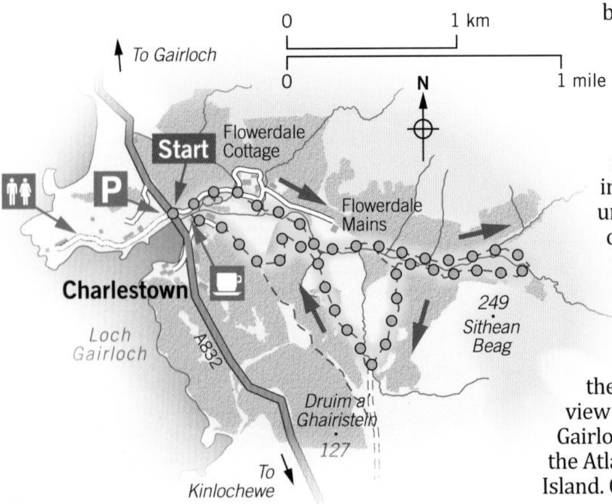

↑ An Groban draws the eye beyond the waterfall

along the path to the next bridge – the turning point of this circuit – the rocky peak of An Groban dominates the skyline. Cross the bridge and turn right, facing that wonderful view again.

The excellent path descends through young trees and heather with high cliffs up to the left, crossing a number of small bridges on its way and dropping through a steep S-bend at one point.

Just before reaching a forest track, there is a memorial to Ian Dall Mackay, the blind piper of Gairloch, a 17th-century musician still held as one of Scotland's greatest pipe composers.

Go left at the junction, now joining the blue markers for the rest of the way. Follow the track as it climbs around the side of the hill, turning right to leave the track and go over a small bridge some distance further on. The bridge is marked by a blue post and these markers continue through the woods on a narrow path. This interesting section of the route provides some lovely views over the glen until you finally reach another track. Turn left onto this then, just 10 yards further on, go right up into the woods, where you'll be reassured you're on the right path when the blue markers return.

This pretty woodland trek is really a bit of a detour, as you end up back on the track further along, but it's worth taking to enjoy the twisty path and in spring it's full of bluebells.

Turn right back onto the track then stay right after a gate to reach a junction with two high gates on the track ahead. Go through both gates to keep to the left fork, rather than following the other track to Flowerdale House. Soon you pass through a small gate to reach the back of the inn a few yards further ahead, and you can cross the stone bridge to return.

WALK 6

Explore a variety of trails around the 'Forest Village'

Grade ❶ Basic route finding required
Distance 6 miles / 10 km
Start/finish Nethy Bridge
Surface Forest and riverside paths and tracks, pavements
Map OS Explorer 403

Taking in a 13th-century castle, a Thomas Telford road bridge and a perfect spot to see red squirrels, this walk has lots to offer.

It starts at the community centre in Nethy Bridge, where there is parking available just up the road from the corner shop. Start by heading down to the main road and crossing the 19th-century Telford bridge and take the first right opposite the hotel.

Head uphill until you see a large white house on the right, opposite which there is a small gate leading into the woods between two properties. Go through the gate and take the path to another gate to meet a clear forest path. Turn left to reach the boundary of a house, then head right through the beautiful pine forest.

Keep to this main path to emerge at a road opposite a school, keeping right and crossing over to take a path to the right of the school grounds. This meets a well-made path that goes left into the woodland, following yellow markers through a gate.

Cross a small burn and go left on a winding way until you reach the next marker post. Leave the yellow route here to go left down to the road, turning right on to it then forking left towards Aultmore a few hundred yards on.

Next, follow the pink Castle Roy Trail which veers left to cross the Allt Mor by a wooden footbridge, following the burn on a little path the other side

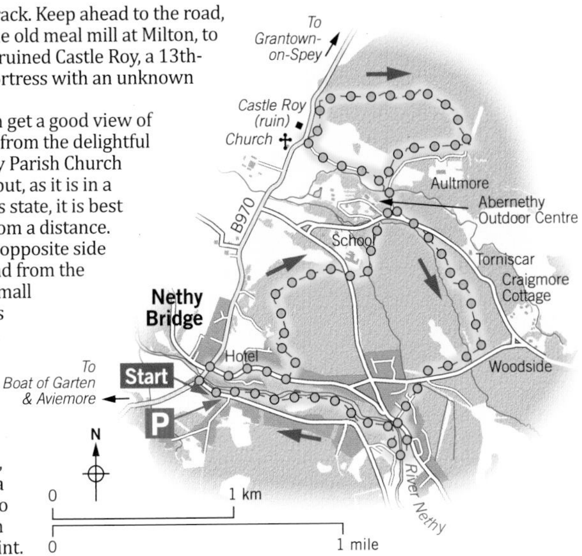

to join a track. Keep ahead to the road, passing the old meal mill at Milton, to reach the ruined Castle Roy, a 13th-century fortress with an unknown history.

You can get a good view of the castle from the delightful Abernethy Parish Church opposite but, as it is in a dangerous state, it is best viewed from a distance.

On the opposite side of the road from the castle, a small path leads to a track, where you turn right to climb through the forest, ignoring a left turn to Grantown at one point.

Beyond the brow of the hill, take a right turn onto a lovely little path at a marker post. This descends past the house at Aultmore and around the edge of the property to emerge at a gate on the track near Milton. Head back over the footbridge to the fork in the road and go left, crossing into the woods by a stile opposite the junction.

The forest path leads left past a lochan and you keep right at a junction further on, going right again as you approach the road to stay inside the boundary fence. When you reach an access point from where the village road sign is clearly visible, leave the forest and cross the road to take a track diagonally right, bypassing a flood by a boardwalk section.

Continue to a T-junction and go left, taking a path right before a telephone box to reach a bridge over the River Nethy. Stay right over the bridge then, after passing a couple of houses, turn right onto the riverside path to enjoy a lovely last kilometre alongside the water and past a red squirrel feeding station.

↖ Castle Roy

← The track from the Allt Mor to Milton

A varied walk to the see the classic Caithness image of the Stacks of Duncansby

Grade 2/3 Exposed coastal walk above high cliffs; navigation skills required for suggested return
Distance 6.5 miles / 11 km
Start/finish John O'Groats
Surface Rocky shore, farmland, clifftop, pathless moor, minor road, tracks; boggy in places
Map OS Landranger 12

Famed as the start or finish of many an end-to-end escapade, John O'Groats offers a classic photo opportunity with its signpost to Land's End, New York and Edinburgh.

Less prominent is the start of a coastal path leading to mainland Britain's most north-easterly point at Duncansby Head, marked by a pair of Caithness standing stones beside the Last House. This varied route follows the straightforward walk between Groats and the lighthouse at Duncansby Head before reaching the famous stacks.

From there you can either return along the coast or, for those with a sense of adventure – and the appropriate skills – continue above the stacks to find an alternative and challenging route back.

The initially stony path was damaged in a storm but is still clear enough to follow and it soon rises onto grazing land, passing through a couple of gates and over a burn by a concrete bridge.

Keep near the shore to pass a rusty winch and reach a bench at a viewpoint overlooking Stroma and the southern Orkney islands, with the high cliffs of Dunnet Head visible on the mainland to the west. Continue to the sandy Sannick Bay, dropping down then climbing the

← Stacks of Duncansby from the south

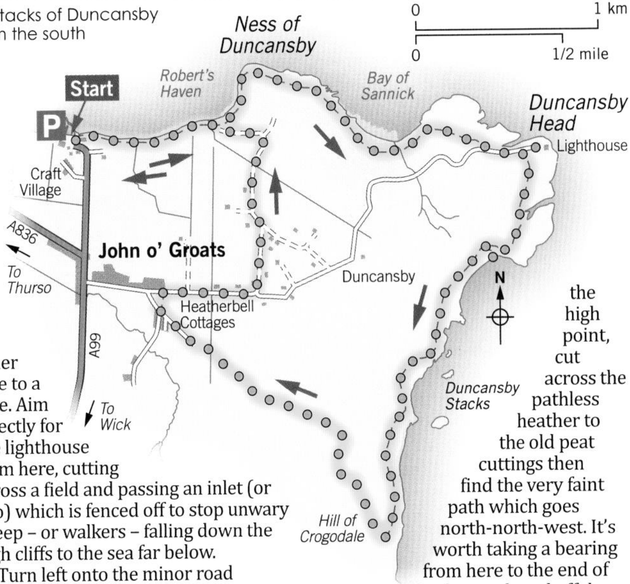

other side to a stile. Aim directly for the lighthouse from here, cutting across a field and passing an inlet (or geo) which is fenced off to stop unwary sheep – or walkers – falling down the high cliffs to the sea far below.

Turn left onto the minor road between Groats and Duncansby Head to reach the lighthouse, built in 1924.

Follow the sign to the Stacks of Duncansby, going via the trig point and past the Geo of Sclaites to meet a fence which overlooks the imposing structures. Go right along the fence and follow it to a gate. Here it's possible to scramble down to sea level with care to gain a different angle of the stacks.

Back on the clifftop continue south down the coast, going through a gate beyond which the cliff edge is not fenced, until you get a closer view of the amazing stacks. Those without navigation skills should return by the outward route from here. Otherwise continue south to reach the spot height at Hill of Crogodale (76m). Just beyond the high point, cut across the pathless heather to the old peat cuttings then find the very faint path which goes north-north-west. It's worth taking a bearing from here to the end of the diagonal road off the Groats-Duncansby Head road.

The going is very rough and boggy over seemingly endless peat cuttings, so it's worth sticking to the high points and detouring around the pits, using the patchy paths and tracks that have been created. Heading roughly north-west, you'll eventually meet a better path. Follow this left and it becomes a soggy but more certain track that soon leads to the road end. Go past the football pitch then cut right to meet the lighthouse road and turn right.

Ignoring a first track left, go left where the stacks walk is signposted right to pass some houses, eventually going left where it enters a field to return to the concrete bridge.

WALK 8

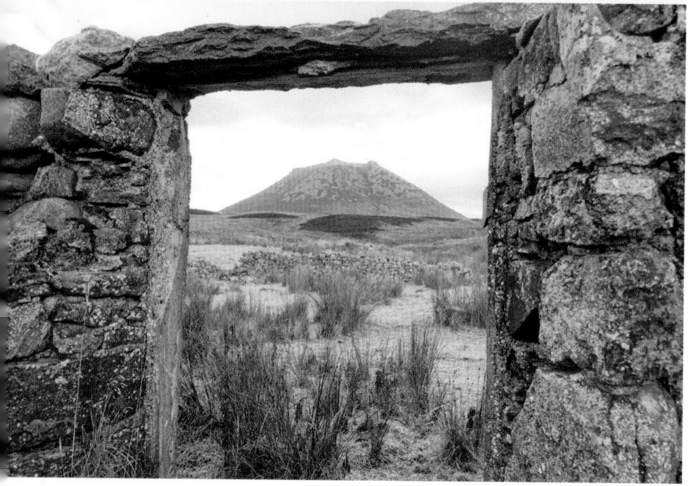

Cycle through the Langwell Estate for an unusual approach to Caithness's highest point

Grade 3 Remote glen with pathless mountain walk
Distance Cycle 16 miles / 26 km return; Walk 5 miles / 8 km
Start/finish Berriedale
Surface Estate track for cycle – rougher towards Wag; boggy pathless mountain and ridges
Map OS Explorer 444

The prominent far north peak of Morven is usually climbed from Braemore, at the end of a minor road from Dunbeath. This longer alternative uses a bike to access the south side of the 706m mountain, riding through the pretty Langwell Estate to reach a ruin at Wag.

From there the walk crosses boggy moor as it heads north around the outside of a forestry plantation to follow the east side of the Allt Preas Bhealaich. It can be tough going across this pathless terrain but it improves as you approach the bealach that connects to Coire Riabhach.

As you approach this col, bear left and cross the burn to gain the east ridge of Morven, where you can pick up a worn path that leads up through the rocks and heather towards the summit.

On a good day you can see for miles across the Flow Country and beyond as you get higher, with the nearby tops of Scaraben and Maiden's Pap prominent in a spectacular view.

From the top, take the more impressive ridge that leads east-north-east off the mountain towards the bealach between Morven and Small Mount. It's possible to include this

lower hill in a longer circuit but this route bears south as it approaches the col, taking the line of the Morven Burn to its junction with the Langwell Water near Wagmore, where there is a ruined farmhouse as well as much older remains of hut circles.

Follow the river back to Wag to pick up the bikes and cycle back to Berriedale, where the ride starts. At the time of writing there is parking available opposite the entrance to the estate, though there are plans to improve the A9 here which could affect this in the future.

The cycle from Berriedale to Wag is fairly straightforward to navigate, following the main track through the estate, passing over the river before leaving the forest by a large gate (the white one to the right of the track is left unlocked).

From here it heads through remote country as it undulates along the line of the river past Aultibea to Wag. It's not technical riding but does require a good degree of fitness to complete the full circuit and ride back out as well.

The reward is a fantastic outing combining cycling and walking in a beautiful part of Caithness and reaching some rarely visited points on the way.

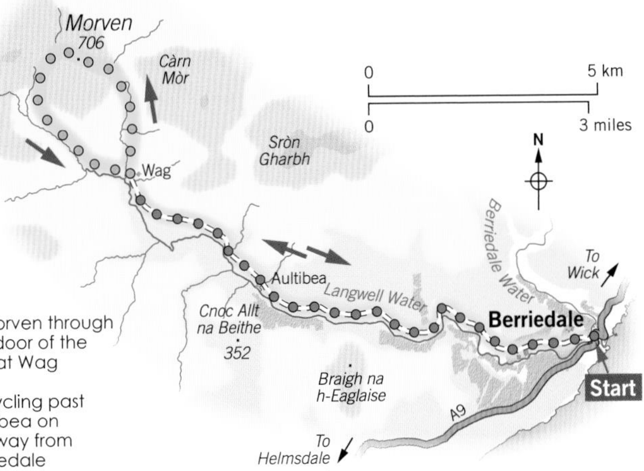

↖ Morven through the door of the ruin at Wag

↗ Cycling past Aultibea on the way from Berriedale

WALK 9

A coastal circuit to a beautiful lighthouse

Grade ❶ Easy to follow and largely flat
Distance 8.75 miles / 14 km
Start/finish Portmahomack
Surface Grass, stony and boggy foreshore; tracks and pavements; minor road. Cattle may be present in places
Map OS Landranger 21; OS Explorer 438

Take your time on this seaside walk and you may be rewarded with wonderful wildlife experiences. Otters can sometimes be seen scurrying in and out of the sandstone bedrock along the coast from Portmahomack while dolphins and whales are worth looking out for from the point at the lighthouse.

There'll also be no shortage of sea birds to see, whatever the conditions. The views are incredible, too – not only to the classic lighthouse when it finally comes into sight but across to the north-east coast on the way there and to Moray on the way back.

Start at the village of Portmahomack, where there's parking available on Main Street and public toilets a short distance away. Continue through the village towards the

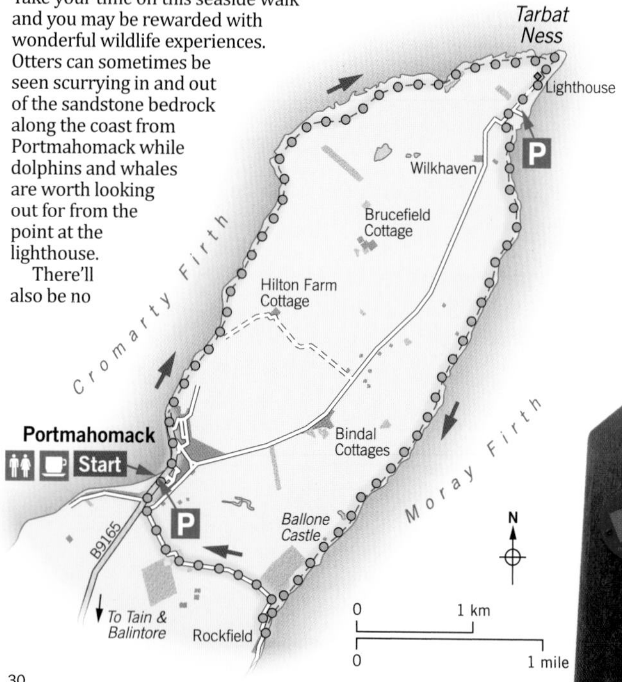

harbour and go past it to a turning point, where you follow a sign to "Tarbatness" between a white wall and the shore.

Go over a stile further on and keep to the obvious path, rough and boggy in places as it stays above the high-water mark and passes through patches of gorse before becoming easier going on soft grass.

Pass an area of sandstone outcrops then stay left of a gate to go narrowly between it and the shore until you reach a stile at the end of the fence, which rusts away into the sea. Stay on the coast past the shack then go right uphill on a clear track to reach a field. Go left through a farm gate then follow the next field along and up to a double gate in the corner.

You can now see the lighthouse across the green fields. From the double gates, follow the diagonal path ahead back towards the sea. Keep to the grass near the coast and stay left of a pond before continuing to beyond the lighthouse until the field edge meets a wall.

Turn right along the wall and go left through a gate at the lighthouse. The houses here are occupied and walkers are asked to stay away from the buildings and to exit by going left of the gas tank in the garden grounds.

You are almost directly under the lighthouse now as you go through a gate onto a track, turning right up to the car park – an alternative starting point for this circuit.

Those with a head for heights may choose to go over the stile to the left at the far side of the car park for a great view of the lighthouse and a narrow path that skirts right, ominously overlooking the high cliffs to the Old Salmon Bothy and the path to

↑ Lighthouse across the rocky shore

Rockfield. To avoid that challenge, stay ahead on the road when you reach the car park and turn left at a T-junction.

The path to Rockfield is signed at a wooden gate. Go through it and past a winch to follow a series of raised beaches along the edge of the sea.

A short way ahead, a marker post directs you up a very steep hill to avoid an eroded area. Follow the second marker left at the top, through a gate then along an earth bank to another post which points straight down a path back to the shore.

The path, boggy and stony in places, eventually heads below the 16th-century Ballone Castle and through a thick area of gorse to the edge of Rockfield, staying close to the sea at all times.

The path emerges right next to a white house in the village, and you walk past its door to emerge at the road end, where you turn immediately right up the steep hill. Follow the minor road over the hill into Portmahomack, going straight over at the give-way junction to cross an area of grass to the bus stop and turn right back to the village centre.

WALK 10

A fine trek among Torridon's giants

Grade ❸ Rises to 600m above sea level and requires mountain walking skills and equipment
Distance 10 miles / 16 km return
Start/finish Coire Dubh Mor car park, Glen Torridon
Surface Well-made stalkers' type path, intermittent path beyond loch outflow
Map Harvey Superwalker, Torridon; OS Explorer 433

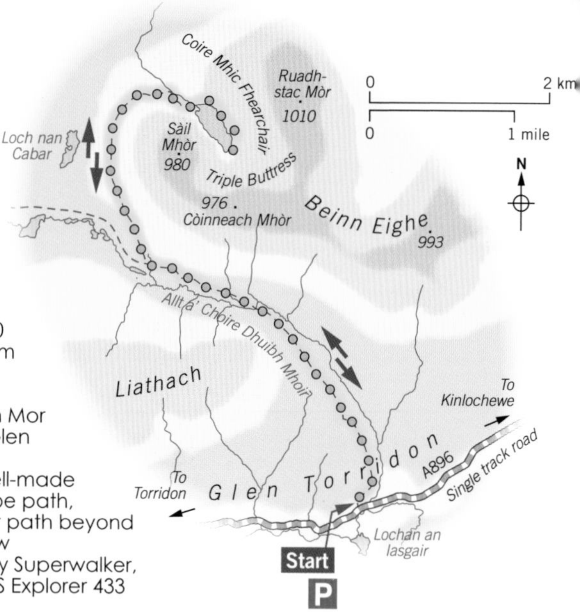

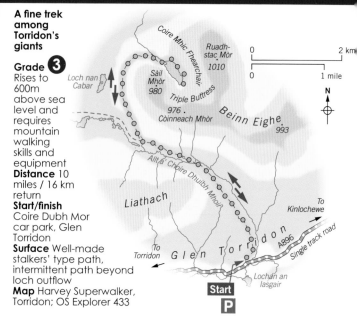

For a real taste of the mountains without having to hit the summits, a walk into the amphitheatre of Coire Mhic Fhearchair takes some beating.

The final reward is a view of the magnificent Triple Buttress of Beinn Eighe, though in clear conditions there is plenty to appreciate throughout the hike from Glen Torridon.

Make no mistake, this is a hillwalking route despite not hitting the ridges of this mountain massif that boasts two Munros – though experienced mountaineers do use this as a popular approach to climb Ruadh-stac Mor and Spidean Coire nan Clach.

The route starts at a popular car park in Glen Torridon at grid reference NG957568, where there is no charge but the National Trust for Scotland does ask for donations for footpath repairs. The paths have improved vastly here in recent years and the trust does a great job of keeping beautiful areas like Torridon accessible without damaging the sense of wildness that attracts people there in the first place.

A Scottish Rights of Way Society sign points to Coire Mhic Nobuil and this walk takes that path from the car park to climb between Liathach and Beinn Eighe, the two giants of the Torridon mountains. The pass between the two crosses the Allt a' Choire Mhoir by a set of stepping stones as you head into the depths of the mountains.

Beinn Dearg, a Corbett tucked away behind the massive slopes of Liathach, comes into view as the gradient eases to reach a cairn at a path junction. Continuing to the left, it is possible to reach Coire Mhic Nobuil beyond the village of Torridon – a fine walk in itself but one that requires transport at either end – but our walk forks right to climb around the lower slope of Sail Mhor.

As you climb higher, more mountains come into view, including Beinn a' Chearcaill, Baosbheinn and Beinn an Eoin. The path swings around the slope until you come close to the Allt Coire Mhic Fhearchair, the burn flowing out of the corrie's loch.

Head uphill to reach the outflow and gain a first glimpse of the Triple Buttress at the back of the corrie, with the giant cliffs of Sail Mhor rising high to the right. To get closer to the buttress, cross the outflow and follow a vague and intermittent path near the east shore of the lochan.

The buttress was the sight of an air crash in March 1951 when a Lancaster bomber struck 15 feet from the top of the cliffs, killing all eight crew members.

Remains of the aircraft can still be found in the area today.

It is said the difficult rescue situation led eventually to the formation of the first mountain rescue teams.

Return the same way.

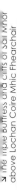

↗ The Triple Buttress and cliffs of Sail Mhor above Lochan Coire Mhic Fhearchair

WALK 11

Reach the pinnacles on this mountain in miniature

Grade ❷ Easy paths but very steep in mountainous territory
Distance 2.5 miles / 4.5 km
Start/finish Stac Pollaidh car park, off road to Achiltibuie
Surface Mountain paths; steep; some loose rock near top
Map Harvey Superwalker: Suilven, Stac Pollaidh & Ben More Assynt

You can see why people want to climb Stac Pollaidh just by looking at it – it's a classic mountain with weather-battered rock crumbling along its crest.

That sandstone ridge may be the playground of scramblers and climbers but the straightforward (if steep) walk to the col is a superb outing in itself.

As far as mountain treks go, this is an easy one. There's a well-constructed path that climbs round the back and up to the summit ridge before dropping back round the front.

The steep plod is no hardship for views that stretch across the north-west Highlands, taking in the Coigach hills, Cul Beag and Cul Mor as well as the unmistakeable Suilven.

There's a purpose-built car park on the road between Drumrunie, north of Ullapool, and Achiltibuie, just below the centre of Stac Pollaidh's distinctive pinnacles. Take the path on the opposite side of the road and go through a gate, climbing on the stone staircase that has been built to reduce the unremitting erosion which was damaging the mountain.

Keep right where the path meets another just before a fence, and

Stac Pollaidh across Loch Lurgainn from Sgurr an Fhidhleir

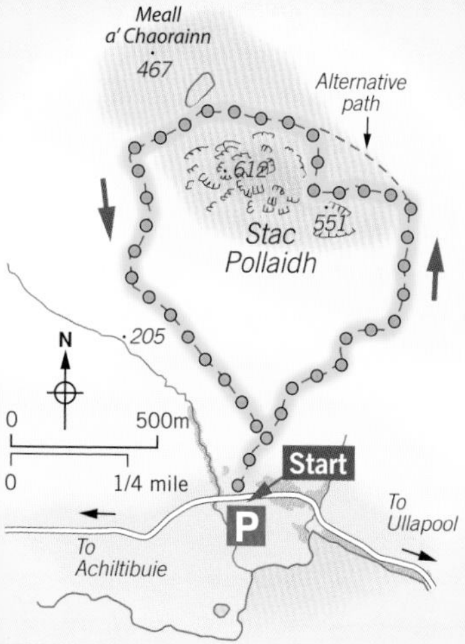

continue through the gate, climbing steeply. Higher up, the crags of the mountain's eastern ridge are close by, and the path rises left to reach a fork a mile from the car park. Keep left to ascend to the ridge, zigzagging the final stretch.

To the left, it's easy to reach the eastern top – but the true summit at the western end of the ridge is another story. This mountain demands a real head for heights and scrambling experience. Don't try it unless you have the skills.

The return route follows an obvious line between the bottom of the crags and a fence, dropping right to meet an alternative path which avoids going to the summit. Where the path splits again, keep to the low one. Follow it down to the fence, going through a gate to meet the initial path.

↑ The author on the track below Saddle Hill

A steep climb to a trig point with views over the Moray Firth

Grade 2 Easy to follow but steep in places
Distance 9 miles / 14.5 km
Start/finish Lay-by off minor road between Craggie and Cawdor at grid ref. NH 766445
Surface Estate tracks with good but rocky surface, very hilly
Map OS Explorer 422

In a commanding position overlooking the Culloden Battlefield and Clava Cairns, Beinn Bhuidhe Mhor is a little-known hill south-east of Inverness.

Its major attraction is the view it offers from its 548m summit, which is easily accessible on good tracks. From the trig point you can see for miles around, over the Beauly and Moray firths and even as far as Suilven in the north-west on a clear day.

A large lay-by offers parking just over a bridge from the start point on the north side of the road. It can be reached from the Culloden Battlefield by following signs down a minor road to the Clava Cairns then, once over the River Nairn, going straight on at a junction then following the road left to pass under the viaduct. Climb a steep hill to the T-junction where you turn right – the lay-by is on the right immediately over the Cassie Burn bridge.

To start the walk, go back over the bridge and turn immediately right onto a vehicle track, following it up a steep section then past a house down a track to the left at Finglack. Stay right here and follow the track right then left to enter the forest through a gate.

Beinn Bhuidhe Mhor

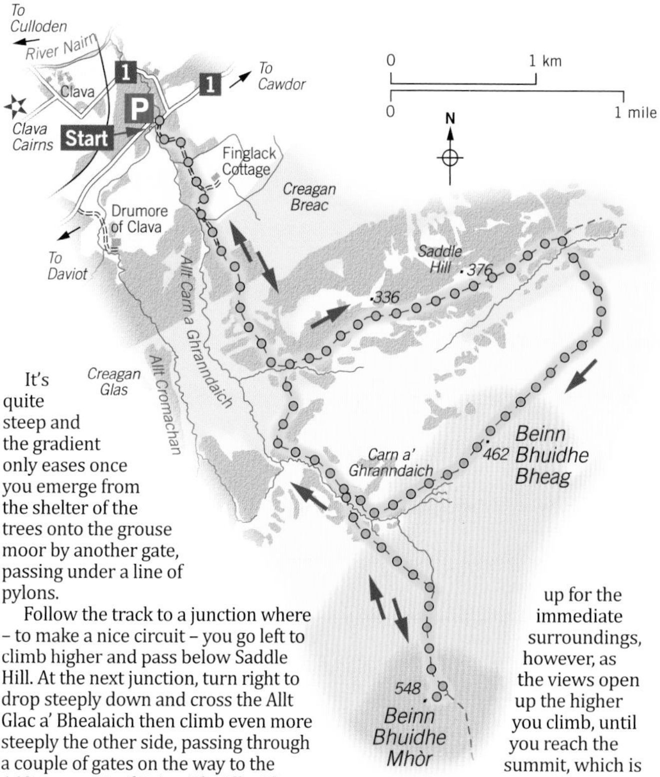

It's quite steep and the gradient only eases once you emerge from the shelter of the trees onto the grouse moor by another gate, passing under a line of pylons.

Follow the track to a junction where – to make a nice circuit – you go left to climb higher and pass below Saddle Hill. At the next junction, turn right to drop steeply down and cross the Allt Glac a' Bhealaich then climb even more steeply the other side, passing through a couple of gates on the way to the 462m summit of Beinn Bhuidhe Bheag.

The top is marked by a large cairn and views to the west can be enjoyed as you descend on the continuing track. This eventually joins the track up to Beinn Bhuidhe Mhor, and you turn sharp left to cross the burn and follow the easy – if not particularly attractive – route up the north side of the hill.

Stopping and looking around makes up for the immediate surroundings, however, as the views open up the higher you climb, until you reach the summit, which is just a short stroll over to your right.

Even though the track continues, it eventually comes to a dead-end, so return the same way to the first junction and keep straight ahead this time, short-cutting the loop over Beinn Bhuidhe Bheag, and go left after fording the Allt Tarsuinn to follow the outward route back to Finglack.

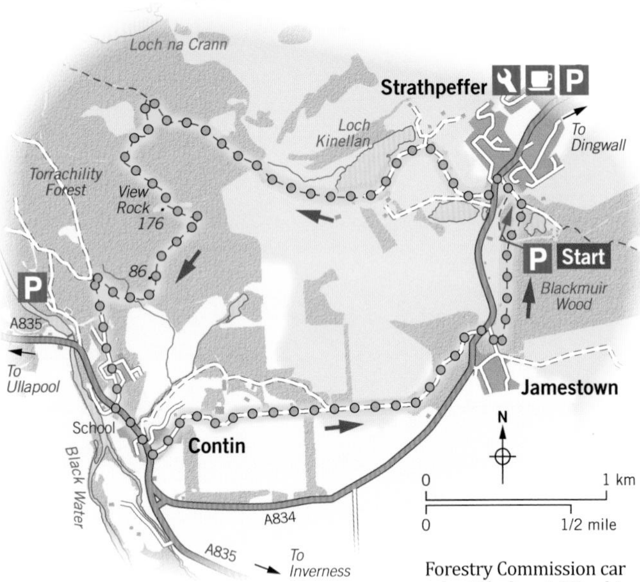

↘ Loch Achility and the Strathconon mountains from View Rock

Excellent tracks and trails lead to a popular viewpoint

Grade ❶ Basic navigation required in places
Distance 5.5 miles / 9 km
Start/finish Blackmuir Wood, Strathpeffer
Surface Forest paths and tracks; pavement
Map OS Explorer 437, Trailmap Strathpeffer

Linking two villages through fine forest trails, returning by a lovely tree-lined track and a long-awaited new section of path, this walk provides plenty of interest. It starts at a Forestry Commission car park at Blackmuir Wood in Strathpeffer – a popular starting point for a walk up the hill fort at Knockfarrel. However, this route goes left out of the car park to return to the road, going left then right at a sign to Kinellan.

Go past the round house at the top of a hill and head left along the track that follows the edge of the beautiful Loch Kinellan. The track climbs beyond the loch and swings right, where you take a track left then a good path off to the left.

Continue into the forest, catching a glimpse of Ben Wyvis through a clearing in the trees, on well-made paths that twist and undulate through this delightful area, which is also

popular with mountain bikers.

A wooden sign points left to View Rock at the bottom of a short downhill section. Follow this upwards past a bench then, at a green marker, divert right to the rock, from which you can see over Loch Achilty to the Strathconon and Fannich mountains in the west.

Keep walking past the rock and stick to the clear path as it winds its way down through a cleared patch of forest and over a new vehicle track. Continue until you reach an obvious fork, where you can cut left to emerge at a gap in a wall which leads out onto another path. If you continue on the right fork, just go left onto the vehicle track and left onto the path between two boulders.

The path skirts around a burn and some rocks to emerge at the end of a road beside some houses. Continue straight down towards the main road, cutting left on a footpath that misses out the final corner to join the start of the pavement beside a bus stop.

Continue through the village (past a shop on the opposite side) until immediately before the fuel station, where you take a track left past a growing number of houses then on to Coul Mains. The tracks swings right round the front of the property and continues beyond between parallel rows of trees. There are good views out over farmland between the trunks on this glorious link to Jamestown. Towards the end of the track, keep left where it joins another track then go straight ahead where the newer track swings left back on itself.

It soon passes a house at a black gate before the main road, where you cross carefully and follow the dead-end road on the other side into Jamestown.

A new path has been created here linking the tiny village with Strathpeffer via Blackmuir Wood and it makes the perfect connection to complete this fine circuit. The path begins just before a ruined church – soon to be converted to a house – on the left towards the end of the road.

A scenic walk through the forest leads back to the car park, staying right where the path splits further on.

→ The tree-lined track at Contin

WALK 14

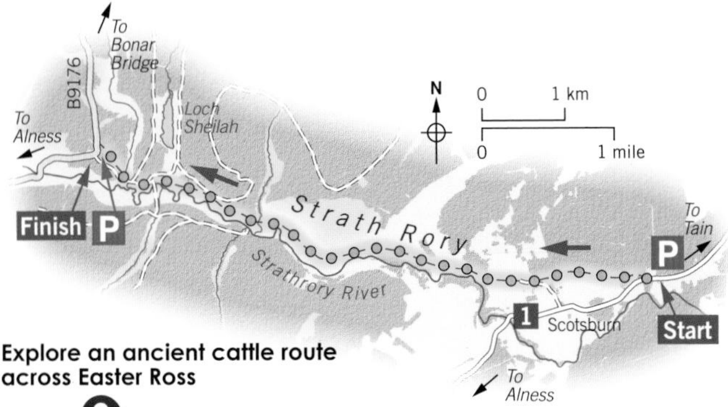

Explore an ancient cattle route across Easter Ross

Grade ❸ Some navigation skills required despite official route
Distance 4.6 miles / 7.5 km
Start/finish Scotsburn, near Tain/Strathrory car park on B9176 Struie road
Surface Forest paths and tracks, farm tracks, grass, heather, bog
Map OS Explorer 438

This former drove road once offered a route to local cattle markets including those at Milton and Kildary – now it's a right of way that takes the intrepid walker into some remote areas.

It may be a recognised route – the Forestry Commission has put up map boards and information along the way – but it is no stroll in the woods. Map and compass are essential, as are some good waterproof boots; there are some seriously boggy sections!

That shouldn't deter you from what is an excellent outing, even better if you can arrange transport at either end of this linear route.

A Scottish Rights of Way Society sign at Dalnaclach, Scotsburn, marks the start of the route, and there is parking here off the single-track road for around four or five cars.

Follow the path onto a vehicle track as it passes a number of houses and continue ahead as the track becomes a narrower path beyond a wooden shed.

This beautiful route runs along the bottom edge of Scotsburn Wood with magnificent views south over the Cromarty Firth. You can see old lichen-covered walls running along parts of the route, as well as mature trees, all of which point to the hidden history of the area.

Shortly, you head behind the rather impressive Scotsburn House on a lovely section then join a muddy track through farmland, following the red markers

↑ A muddy track leads to a deserted croft house at Coag as you head deeper into the hills

ahead through a gate. After a short climb through some deciduous trees, you can hear the river far below but you can't see it just yet.

The track descends to an open grassy area at Coag with a deserted croft house at the far end of it. Beyond that, there seem to be just trees for miles on end as you become aware of how far away from civilisation you are getting.

Turn right immediately after the fence just beyond the house to follow the red marker across a very faint path through the heather.

The soggy path soon meets a more obvious (though even wetter) track heading towards Cnoc an Duin – the hill rising up ahead of you – and skirts below it. This area is on the fringe of a Site of Special Scientific Interest, with much of the riverside area protected because it is home to a substantial remnant of ancient native pine forest, which is also host to the elusive capercaillie.

Coming round the edge of Cnoc an Duin, which has an unfinished fort on its top, there's a great view through the Scots pine and birch ahead to the Struie, and you can now see the Strathrory River below.

Going over a series of boardwalks, head down to the river and follow it west between the water and the fenced forest up to the right. Cross a tributary by a wooden footbridge then follow a clearer path to join a track after a metal gate. Follow it ahead then uphill to the car park on the Struie road.

WALK 15

Take a stroll by the river on a gentle forest walk

Grade ❶ Waymarked walk
Distance 3.5 miles / 5.5 km
Start/finish River Oich car park, Auchteraw, near Fort Augustus
Surface Forest tracks, woodland and grass riverside paths
Map OS Explorer 400

You can really get close to the water on this meandering route beside the River Oich, a stretch of water that links Loch Ness with the less famous but no less attractive Loch Oich.

The Caledonian Canal, engineered by Thomas Telford in the late 19th century, runs parallel to the river but remains tantalisingly out of sight for the duration of this walk.

It begins at a Forestry Commission car park at Auchteraw, a couple of miles from Fort Augustus in the Great Glen. Follow the marker post onto the river walk which leads you down a path into the woods.

Turn right almost immediately, following the yellow route through birch wood as it winds over a small bridge and up to reach a vehicle track. Go left and follow the track around to the right. For now you are at a distance from the river, with the return route taking you much closer.

Continue ahead where the green route splits to the right and cross a bridge over the Auchteraw Burn to continue into a wooded area.

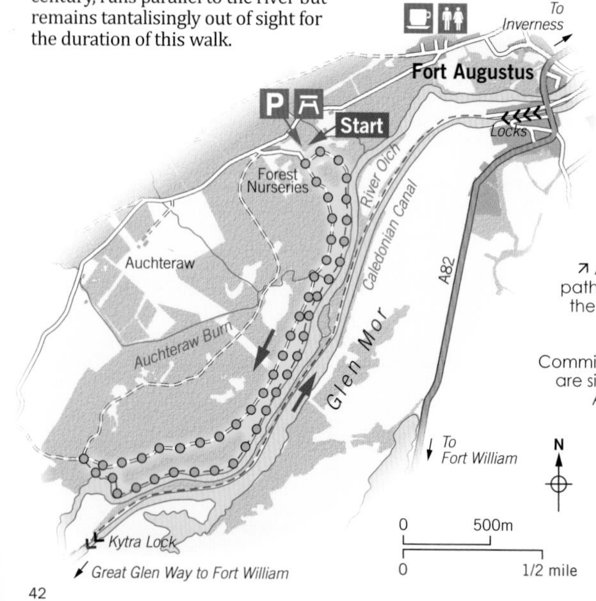

↗ A beautiful path alongside the River Oich

→ Forestry Commission walks are signed from Auchteraw

There's a lovely pine forest section beyond here as the track continues to a junction. Go left here to join a path through the forest to the riverside.

Following the river downstream, the path traces a few big bends in the watercourse before passing through a nice wooded area and emerging onto grass beside the water.

Stick closely to the river for a while now on the clear path – well used by walkers and anglers – as it alternates between open areas and woodland sections with a few benches here and there.

Approaching the Auchteraw Burn again, you turn away from the water to cross this tributary by a nice little wooden bridge before returning to the main river – all well signed with the yellow markers.

After a narrow stretch of path, move away from the river to cross a boardwalk and climb uphill briefly, keeping right as you meet another path and following an old stone wall back to the car park.

WALK 16

Discover an unspoilt golden beach in a far-flung corner of the Highlands

Grade 2/3 Good track/path out to bay; return route follows sometimes vague path close to cliff edges, care required
Distance 10 miles / 16 km
Start/finish Blairmore car park, west of Kinlochbervie
Surface Vehicle track, stepping stones, well-made path, sand, steep grass/stone/dirt path, pathless heather hillside, boggy
Map OS Landranger 9

This mesmerising bay which stretches for more than 2km along the coast is the last place in Britain where a mermaid was reportedly spotted. I've never seen such a being at Sandwood – or anywhere else for that matter – but the place certainly has a beauty and charm all of its own.

This is one walk not to be missed, however remote it may seem.

A good track and path leads the 4.5 miles from the car park at Blairmore, which you can reach by following minor roads beyond Kinlochbervie. There are toilets here as well as a tap providing drinking water.

The track is signed from the road to Sandwood (though vehicles are no longer allowed). Cross the stile at the gate and follow the track past Loch na Gainimh, using the obvious shortcut above the loch if you like.

The landscape here is of barren and boggy moor but, looking back, the dominant slopes of Foinaven and Arkle can be seen.

Stepping stones offer walkers a dry way around a lochan that spills onto the track before you reach the end of the vehicle track above Loch a' Mhuilinn. From here the John Muir Trust – which owns the land – has created an excellent path that continues past the loch and climbs a little past a couple more lochs to the right.

At a post, the path bears left to drop

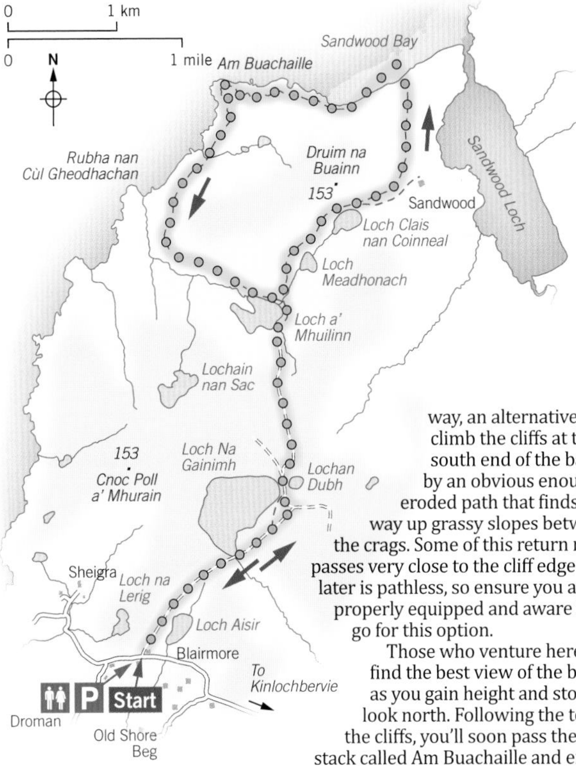

← Looking north over Sandwood Bay

down towards the bay and the view north along the cliffs is spectacular. As you descend onto grass, keep right on the clearest path through the dunes to follow a sandy path onto the beach.

You may want to allow time to explore this huge expanse of golden sand or to enjoy a picnic before finding your way back.

If you don't want to return the same way, an alternative is to climb the cliffs at the south end of the bay by an obvious enough eroded path that finds its way up grassy slopes between the crags. Some of this return route passes very close to the cliff edge and later is pathless, so ensure you are properly equipped and aware if you go for this option.

Those who venture here will find the best view of the bay as you gain height and stop to look north. Following the top of the cliffs, you'll soon pass the sea stack called Am Buachaille and enjoy some fine coastal scenery.

Where the land drops the other side of Carn an Righ, bear left on vague paths through the heather to follow the line of the burn which runs out of Loch a' Mhuilinn. Stay on the north side of the burn, dropping down to meet the shore of the loch where you can pick up a clearer path that leads back to the outward route.

WALK 17

Out-and-back route with a long look over Loch Ness

Grade ❶ Long walk but largely on forest tracks
Distance 14 miles / 22 km
Start/finish Invermoriston
Surface Forest tracks and minor road, hilly
Map OS Explorer 416; OS Landranger 34

From the start of this walk to the summit of Sron na Muic – which translates as the nose of the pig from the Gaelic – the distance is only around a mile, as the crow flies. However, it's a little more difficult to reach than that.

Getting to the communications mast on top of the hill overlooking Loch Ness and the Great Glen involves seven miles of walking on minor roads and, mostly, forestry tracks. If you've got a bike with decent gears (and plenty of power in your legs) it's also possible to cycle the whole way.

The reward comes from the outlook at the top, as you glimpse the loch nearly 500 metres below. It's also a very peaceful walk, with fewer people venturing up here than tackling the lower-level walks suggested on a notice board in the car park at Invermoriston.

Turn left out of the car park and cross the river by the main road bridge, going right on a dead-end road towards Dalcataig on the route of the Great Glen Way.

Ignore a marker post for the Great Glen Way pointing left into a cleared area of forest and continue on the road, which leads to a forestry gate further on. Continue ahead as another marker points left – this is a remnant of the now defunct Great Glen Cycle Route – and follow the line of the River Moriston as it tumbles through a series of mini rapids below.

As the track starts to climb, stay left at a fork to keep going uphill and soon cross a new bridge. Continue ahead where a track goes left (marked as a

↑ Looking back to the forest from the approach to the summit

crossroads on the OS map) then take a left turn at the next junction, following the track round to the right – ignoring a grassy track ahead – to climb higher.

Fabulous views begin to open up now down Glen Moriston and over the Strath Cluanie. A hairpin left bend offers a great viewpoint but there's still some climbing to do yet.

Fork left immediately after the bend and enjoy a break in the gradient as the track contours round the side of the hill through the trees. You soon start to climb again and eventually reach the edge of the forest, from where it's about a mile on a twisting track to the communications mast and – more importantly – the fine views.

Looking down the glen you can see over Fort Augustus to the Corrieyairack Pass and even over Loch Oich to Loch Lochy. To the north you get an unusual view of Meall-fuar Mhonaidh – the prominent hill on the west side of Loch Ness not far from Drumnadrochit.

All the effort of the climb seems worthwhile now – and the added bonus is that it's all downhill from here.

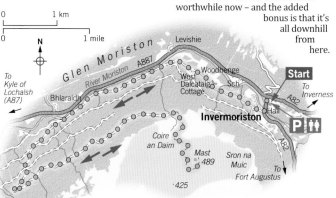

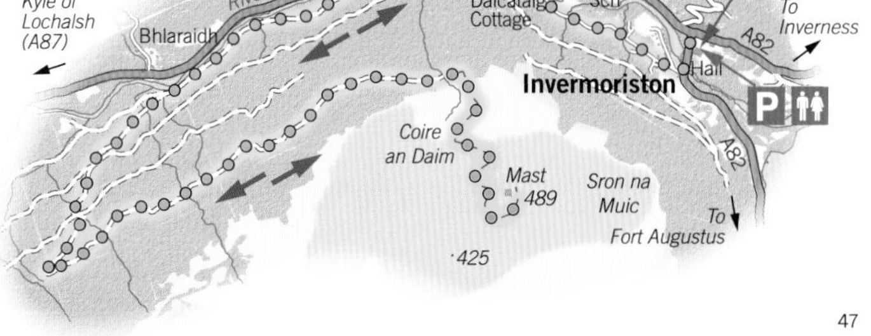

WALK 18

Wade sight stone at Slochd ↑

Follow in Wade's footprints on this circuit over the Slochd

Grade ❷ Involves some road walking and potentially dangerous crossing of A9
Distance 7 miles / 11 km
Start/finish Tomatin
Surface Minor road, cycle track, crossing of A9 at Slochd summit, vehicle tracks across grouse-shooting moor
Map OS Explorer 417

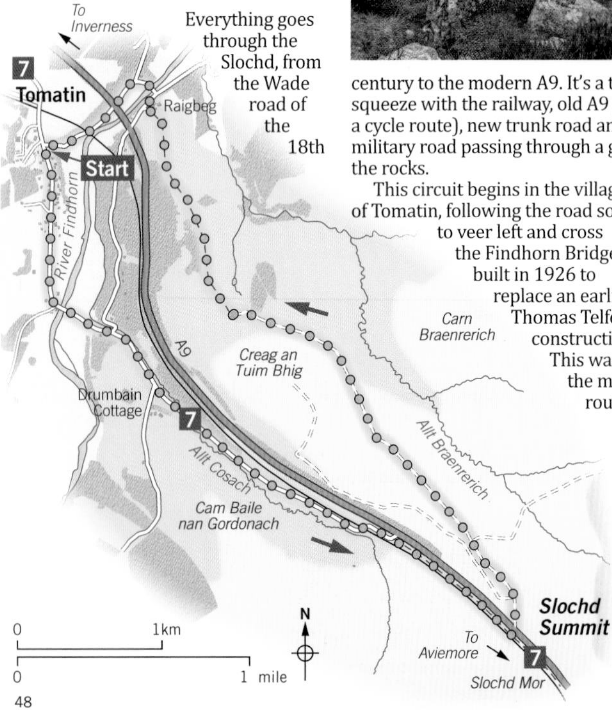

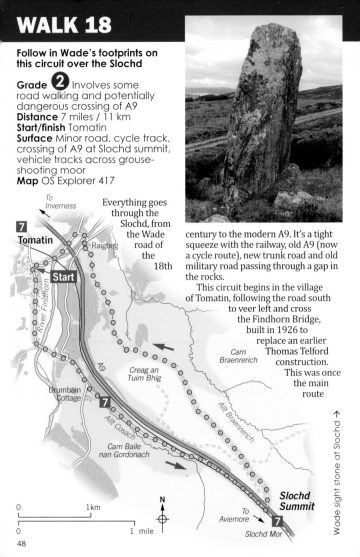

Everything goes through the Slochd, from the Wade road of the 18th century to the modern A9. It's a tight squeeze with the railway, old A9 (now a cycle route), new trunk road and old military road passing through a gap in the rocks.

This circuit begins in the village of Tomatin, following the road south to veer left and cross the Findhorn Bridge, built in 1926 to replace an earlier Thomas Telford construction. This was once the main route north but traffic is fairly light down here nowadays. There's no pavement as the road climbs alongside a forest then crosses the railway shortly before a junction with the A9. Just before the junction, take a right turn onto a cycle track that runs beside the railway line, where a large sign marks the top.

An old relic of the earlier road is also visible on the opposite carriageway in the form of a rusty and broken sign marking the 1,332ft summit.

After the railway sign turn left and take extreme care crossing the busy A9 to meet a track on the far side. At a new gate, a Scottish Rights of Way Society sign marks the return route to Tomatin.

Go through the gate and up the track to a large standing stone. This is an original sight line marker stone from the period of construction of the military road. Bear left at the stone to follow the main track along the right of way to Raigbeg, ignoring a number of other tracks leading away from the main route.

The feeling is very different here as the road section of the walk comes to an end and you can enjoy being well away from the hustle and bustle as you walk through this heather moorland.

Further on, pass through a gate and follow a grassy stretch to a junction, taking the right turn to drop down through forestry with views over the River Findhorn to Raigbeg. On reaching the houses, skirt right then left to meet the minor road below at a sign pointing back to Slochd.

Turn right onto the road then go left to cross a wooden bridge over the river towards Tomatin. This road loops left on its way there to pass under the huge bridges that carry the modern A9 and the railway over the Findhorn valley.

Walking under the railway viaduct over the Findhorn

WALK 19

Climb to a monument with a distinctly Indian flavour

Grade ❶ Straightforward navigation on popular paths
Distance 4.5 miles / 7 km
Start/finish Jubilee Path car park on road to Boath, near Alness
Surface Paths and forest tracks, rough and very boggy in places
Map OS Explorer 438

The monument on top of Fyrish Hill, a representation of the Gate of Negapatam in Madras in India, is worth the steep walk up to for the views alone.

It must have been a fair task for the people of Fyrish to move these massive stones up the hill to the 453m (1,486ft) summit once, never mind the second time as the myth suggests.

The monument was built on the orders of Sir Hector Munro of Novar in 1782. The story goes that due to the lands being cleared for sheep, he wanted to provide employment for the local people, so ordered its construction. To pay them twice, he apparently had the stones rolled back down the hill so they could continue in their work.

The walk begins at a signposted car park on the minor road to Boath, a left turn off the B9176 Struie road if heading north.

The well-marked Jubilee Path leads away from the single-track road into the lovely woodland. Keep ahead at first then continue straight ahead at a crossroads of tracks, following the obvious wooden marker poles with white arrows.

The path then drops on a series of stone steps to cross the Contullich Burn over

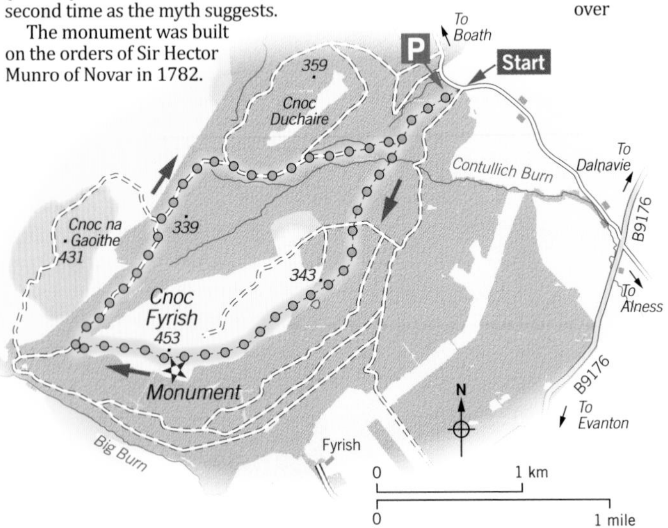

↑ The Fyrish Monument overlooking the Cromarty Firth

a small gorge by a wooden bridge. Stone steps rise again the other side where you continue on the clear track, which begins to climb more steeply. Go straight on at another crossroads further ahead.

Pass a small lochan on your left then continue to the monument, from where there are fantastic views across the Cromarty Firth to the Black Isle and beyond.

A sign points back the same way to the car park but, for an alternative return, continue on the track past the monument, which turns very rocky and bumpy down the ridge of the hill. Turn right at a T-junction to enter the interesting forest, which is boggy underfoot in places but worth it for the varied scenery on the way back.

At the next junction, go right and continue until you meet the circuitous track around Cnoc Duchaire, where you go right just after crossing a small burn.

Ignore a grassy track off to the left further ahead, then stay on the right fork at a muddy junction.

As you descend here, look out for a crossroads and turn left, now back on the Jubilee Path which you follow all the way back to the road.

Waterfalls and woodland on a twisting circuit through the trees

Grade 2 Clear if intricate series of paths
Distance 2.75 miles / 4.5 km
Start/finish Big Burn car park, off A9 at north end of Golspie
Surface Riverside paths including steps and bridges, short section on quiet road
Map OS Explorer 441

Hidden waterfalls and a series of intricate woodland paths make this a fascinating circuit of the Big Burn at Golspie.

The walk starts at the north end of the village, where there's a car park behind the stonemason's next to the Golspie Inn. A rusty sign points you to the waterfall along a well-made path, which soon reaches an arched bridge across the burn. The bridge is dedicated to Colin Ploughman, who came to the area during World War II to fell timber for the war effort and who more recently voluntarily cleared trees to help keep the Big Burn walk accessible.

Continue under the massive railway bridge alongside the burn then cut right through a picnic area and cross a number of tributaries as the path meanders further inland. Go left where a tiny coloured signpost at ground level hides beside a bench and keep to the path nearest the burn.

Soon you'll reach one of the highlights of this wonderful little route, a series of footbridges that take you to and fro across the Golspie Burn through a narrow, rocky gorge.

The first few bridges take you over the burn then back again, with a pretty waterfall fanning down from the far side, spraying you as you get nearer.

The path then cuts left, crossing the burn again in the tight gap, continuing upstream for a short distance then crossing yet again. Go left to cross back almost immediately then, at the far side of the bridge, detour right along the narrow path and boardwalk which leads to the bottom of the main waterfall on the burn.

Returning to the bridge, go right and climb up the steps that take you to the top of the waterfall, where you can look over the edge if you dare! Turn left and the path follows the burn and, at one point, almost merges with the upper path – part of the return route – but for now stay left closest to the burn. Just as you can see a house ahead, another bridge leads you left across the water once more and then a path climbs up from a bench to meet the minor road.

Turn right onto the road and follow it round a sharp left-hand bend down to the bridge. Cross it and turn right through a little gate, staying immediately left of the track that leads to the house. There are fantastic views from this path, ahead through the trees and over the burn to the Duke of Sutherland monument on top of Ben Bhraggie.

You'll skirt close to the path you met earlier before passing the Backies road car park – another possible starting point for this walk. Down to your right beyond here a hollow holds a forest of trees lathered in lichen and the view overlooks the Moray Firth.

Ahead, you can enjoy a circuit of the small lochan before heading down the steps which lead to the junction with the ground-level signpost. Bear left to return to the start.

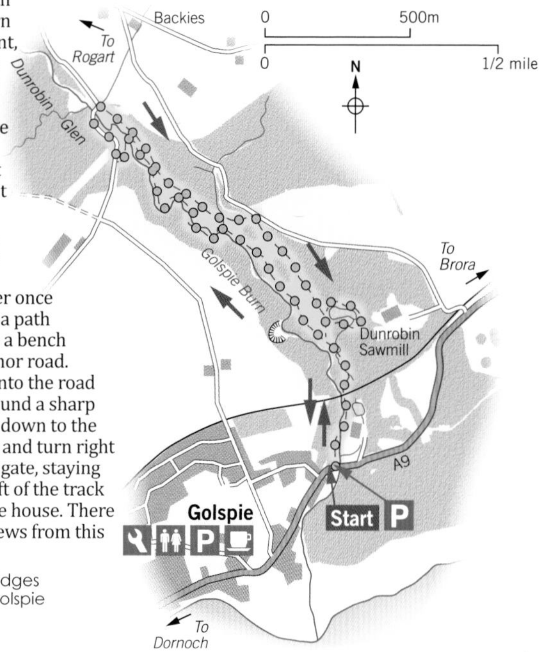

⇖ A series of bridges crisscross the Golspie Burn through a narrow gorge

Head into the wilds on a ride into the unknown

Grade 3 Remote and rough
Distance 36 miles / 58 km
Start/finish Muir of Ord
Surface Minor road; tarmac track; rough vehicle track; forest track, very boggy in places
Map OS Landranger 26

Looking at my most worn OS map, this track across the hills from Glen Orrin to Struy yells out to be explored. It's no easy ride across some rough and remote terrain but it's a real adventure to be enjoyed rather than endured.

There's even a bothy part-way round looked after by the Hydro, which is well worth a visit – especially if the weather takes a turn for the worse!

The ride starts tamely enough, leaving Muir of Ord by crossing the railway bridge and turning left towards the Glen Ord distillery. Go left on a minor road to Aultgowrie, which climbs gradually before crossing the Allt Goibhre and reaching a small group of houses.

Immediately before a second bridge, go left onto a surfaced track over a cattle grid to enter the Fairburn Estate. The tarmac track leads to the

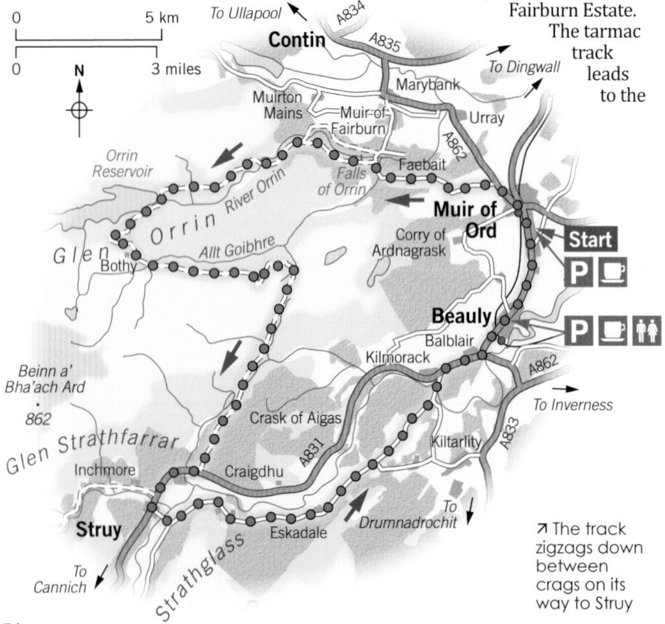

↗ The track zigzags down between crags on its way to Struy

Orrin Reservoir dam, a straightforward start to the off-road part of the route.

Keep left where a track joins from the right and go through the gate ahead. After a plank bridge over the River Orrin you climb into the hills and eventually reach the dam, from where there are fine views of the Strathfarrar mountains over the water.

There's a second dam round the corner which you cross before the tarmac ends and a stiff climb welcomes you to the rough stuff – though it's still decent for mountain biking at this point. Route finding is easy as you follow the track, but it can be exposed up here and the only shelter is a small bothy by the trackside.

The surface stays reasonable through Gleann Goibhre until a ford over a tributary of the Allt Goibhre, from where it really deteriorates. The track bends right to pass Loch Ballach before a long, steep descent on potentially slippery ground. Take care on the way down to Lochan Fada and the forest below as the track zigzags between crags to eventually reach a gate at the forest.

The fun still isn't over, though, as the forest track is, in my experience, pretty awful too! Be prepared to negotiate flooded sections of it on foot until the surface improves, then it's a lovely ride down to Forest Cottage and the road ahead.

Go right to cross the stone bridge to Struy then turn left after the inn to cross the River Glass. Take a left turn to follow the magnificent minor road up Strathglass. At Hughton take a left to climb over Finellan and down the other side, going left at a junction to cross the River Beauly and meet the A831, turning right towards Beauly. On reaching the A862, go left through Beauly then continue to Muir of Ord.

CYCLE 2

Explore the beautiful Coigach peninsula on the magnificent north-west coast

Grade 2 Hilly route
Distance 48 miles / 77 km
Start/finish Ullapool/Lochinver
Surface A-road section to start followed by single-track roads the rest of the way
Map OS Landranger 15 & 19

Take your bike on the bus for a day trip to remember. This is more than a bike route – it's a whole adventure.

Starting at Inverness, the Highland Bike Bus will drop you at Ullapool and collect you at Lochinver, giving you around six-and-a-half hours to complete this ride.

Beginning at the pier at Ullapool, it heads north and into the Coigach peninsula, passing below Stac Pollaidh before enticing the rider with views over the beautiful Summer Isles as it loops into Achiltibuie. It then meanders through the Inverpolly nature reserve with views ahead to the magnificent Suilven before dropping into Lochinver Bay.

From the pier at Ullapool, go straight up the hill and follow signs for the A835 North. At the main road, go left and follow it through Ardmair and Strathcanaird.

After climbing out of this strath, there is a viewpoint at a layby looking west over Coigach – the name translates from the Gaelic as "the five Achs", as the land was divided into fifths: Achnahaird, Achlochan, Acheninver, Achabhraighe and Achduart – to the crumbling rocks of Stac Pollaidh (see Walk 11).

Turning left at a junction at Drumrunie – signposted for Achiltibuie – you follow an amazing single-track road that twists and winds its way north-west, passing directly below Stac Pollaidh. You soon pass the

The winding road between Achiltibuie and Lochinver

turn-off to Lochinver, which gives you the option to shorten the full route at this stage – but it would mean missing out on a great circuit of the peninsula and a visit to the seaside village of Achiltibuie.

So continue past the junction and beyond Loch Osgaig to a T-junction next to a parking area. Turn right to follow the loop anti-clockwise.

The road climbs up past a turning to the gorgeous golden beach at Achnahaird to a viewpoint slightly beyond the summit. This overlooks the Summer Isles and is a great place to just sit and appreciate the beauty of the area.

Drop downhill and go left after a cattle grid through Altandhu and Polbain and alongside a long beach to a give-way junction. Head right to visit Achiltibuie, which has a hotel and a grocer's shop, with a youth hostel further along the dead-end road.

Returning to this junction, keep right, going past lochs Vatachan and Raa then turning right towards Ullapool at the parking area. On reaching the Lochinver turn-off, follow it left and climb uphill. This twisting, turning, rising and dipping road is great fun as it snakes its way north with great views to Suilven in places.

After crossing the River Kirkaig and going through Strathan, the road finally drops into Lochinver, where you'll find plenty of options for refreshments while you wait for the bus.

➲ The Highland Bike Bus is operated by DE Coaches and runs from Inverness to Durness during the summer. For timetable and booking details, visit www.inverness-durness-highland-bike-bus.co.uk or call 01463 222444.

Mysterious Caithness stones on a varied and fascinating trail

Grade 1 Some rough surfaces on forest tracks
Distance 10.5 miles / 17 km
Start/finish Camster Forest car park, ½ mile south of Camster Cairns on Lybster-Watten road
Surface Forest tracks, boggy in places; minor roads; short stretch on main road
Map OS Landranger 11

The excellently named Hill O' Many Stanes is thought by some to be a Bronze Age lunar observatory. It's a curious idea and stargazers would have no problems taking in the night sky from here even today given the lack of street lighting in many parts of the far north.

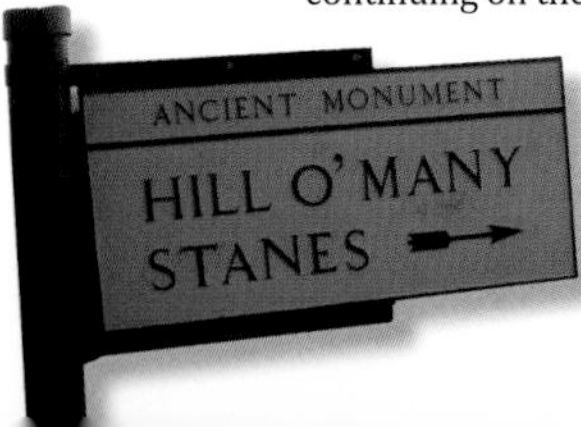

By day, it's worth following the Camster cycle trail through the forest to the hill at Mid Clyth, returning by one of the straightest – and greatest – roads I've ever ridden on.

A small parking area is tucked away at the edge of a forest plantation half a mile south of the Cairns of Camster, a site of well-preserved Neolithic chambered cairns, on a minor road most easily accessed from Lybster on the A99.

Enter the forest on bikes by continuing on the track, which bends left then right over a low gate. It can be boggy in this artificial-looking forest but you're likely to get a peaceful ride as it climbs very

← Cyclists on the straight Lybster-Watten road

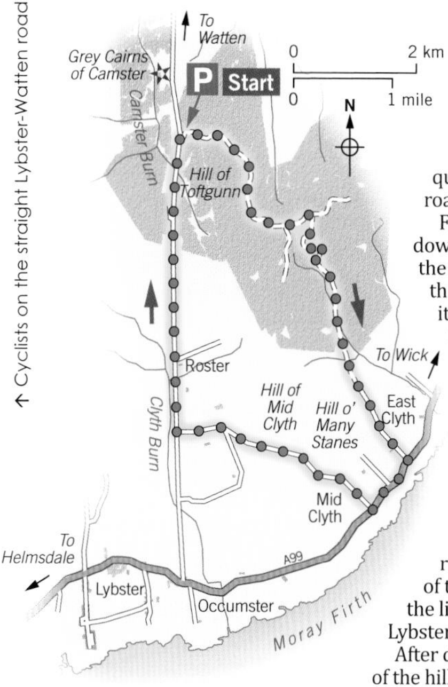

After the top of the hill there's a long descent which requires care in places on the rough and sometimes boggy track which emerges from the forest at a gate.

Go straight ahead past a quarry and farm to meet the road ahead.

From here it's an easy ride down to near the coast, passing the "Ancient Monument" sign to the Hill O' Many Stanes, where it's worth stopping to take a look at the 22 parallel rows of standing stones – and the view from this prominent situation.

Continue to the junction with the A99 and turn right onto that road, taking the next signposted road right to Camster.

A fabulous single-track road goes over the shoulder of the hill at Mid Clyth, crossing the line of the former Wick and Lybster Light Railway.

After dropping down the other side of the hill, turn right at the T-junction at Laid and follow the Camster road north towards the forest.

gradually. Stick to the obvious track throughout the forestry part of the ride, staying left at a fork after a couple of miles and going right at the top of the hill where an older track continues straight on.

A short detour around half a mile each way takes you past the car park to the Cairns of Camster, where there are paths and trails around this fascinating site.

The long cairn at the Cairns of Camster

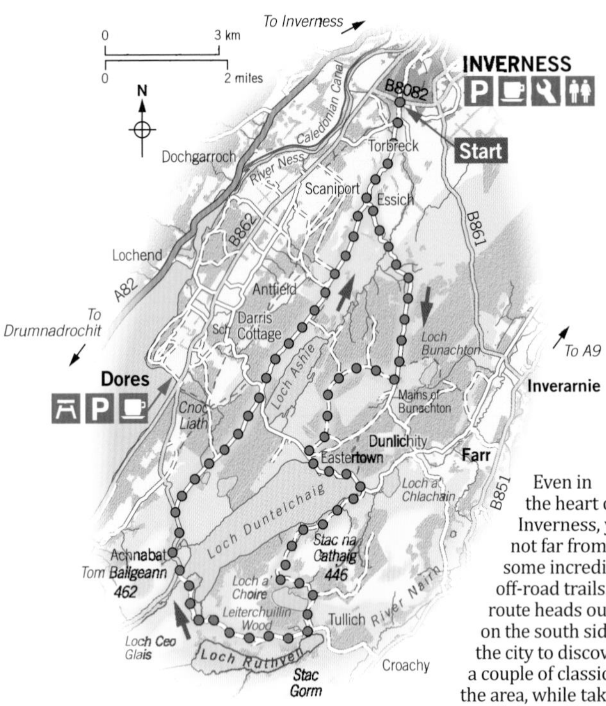

→ A cairn marks the summit of the pass between Duntelchaig and Ruthven

Exploring off-road trails close to the Highland capital

Grade 2 Some hills and a rough, fairly remote track
Distance 25 miles / 40 km
Start/finish Essich roundabout, Inverness (B8082)
Surface Minor roads, forestry and vehicle tracks, muddy and hilly
Map OS Landranger 26

Even in the heart of Inverness, you're not far from some incredible off-road trails. This route heads out on the south side of the city to discover a couple of classics in the area, while taking in some equally beautiful quiet stretches of road.

The route rises to 370m above sea level, so there's a fair amount of climbing involved, but the equal amount of downhill and fabulous tracks will stick in your mind much more than any effort required. It's a true adrenaline-pumping ride that's short enough for a Sunday morning or even a midsummer's evening.

Starting at the Essich roundabout on the B8082 southern distributor

road, take the minor road south below the power lines and past the houses to start climbing the hill towards Essich. It's a long climb up towards Loch Ashie but the quiet road is great for riding and you are quickly away from the city.

Take a left turn towards Bunachton immediately after a house at Essich and climb past the electricity sub-station until the gradient eases across the moor. After passing the Mains of Bunachton, look out for a metal gate across a track on your right – follow this track past a ruin to another gate at the entrance to Loch Ashie Forest.

Take the left fork through the woodland and keep to the main track, watching out for a fence across the track close to where it emerges near Loch Duntelchaig. The fence is difficult to see from a speedy bike so go carefully, using the stile just left of the track to cross before descending the final stretch to the road.

There's a fine view over the loch from here as you turn left to follow a spectacular single-track road that hugs the edge of the loch.

After passing the end of the water, leave the road for a track on the right (just before a long lay-by) that leads to the outlet works. This is one of my favourite parts of the route as it follows the shore of the loch before climbing gradually past a house at Leiterchullin then stays left to go through hairpin bends and reach the summit of the pass, marked by a cairn.

The view is spectacular and the steep descent is, too! Take care as you follow the main track, going straight ahead after a sharp right-hand bend at one point to drop to the road above Loch Ruthven.

Go right onto the road as it leads you away from the loch, descending through a series of S-bends after Dalcrombie before crossing the causeway at the south end of Loch Duntelchaig. A short steep climb leads to a junction where you turn right onto the B862, taking the next right, signed to Inverness.

Go straight on at the crossroads then enjoy a long descent overlooking the Moray Firth as you return to Essich.

CYCLE 5

Explore delightful coastal villages on a scenic circuit

Grade ❶ Straightforward but attention required to follow cycle route in places
Distance 18 miles / 29 km
Start/finish Cullen beach
Surface Minor roads, tarmac and stone cycle path, short stretch on main road
Map Aberdeen to Shetland (NCN1) published by Sustrans, plus free Sustrans leaflet, Go Traffic Free in Scotland, Firth of Tay to Moray

The spectacular viaduct which curves over the rooftops of Cullen is a fine backdrop to the start and finish of this family-friendly cycle.

The reason this eye-catching piece of engineering exists is simple – the local landowner didn't want the railway going near Cullen House so it had to go close to the coast.

From the beach car park beside the golf course, cross the burn by a low bridge and follow the road towards the harbour, turning sharp right up a hairpin bend to pass the Bayview Hotel. Continue up Seafield Street to join the main road, where you go under the arch before turning right at the square onto Grant Street.

Join National Cycle Network Route 1 by taking the second left up South Deskford Street, forking right at the top and continuing to meet the B9018.

Turn right here to pass Lintmill – where you leave Route 1 and instead continue on the B road for just over 2km until a right turn on a left-hand bend signed for Hill of Maud.

This quiet road undulates in and out of a few forest plantations as it climbs through beautiful countryside to a T-junction, from where the ride is mostly downhill or flat. Turn right to

Bow Fiddle Rock and (above) the viaduct in Cullen.

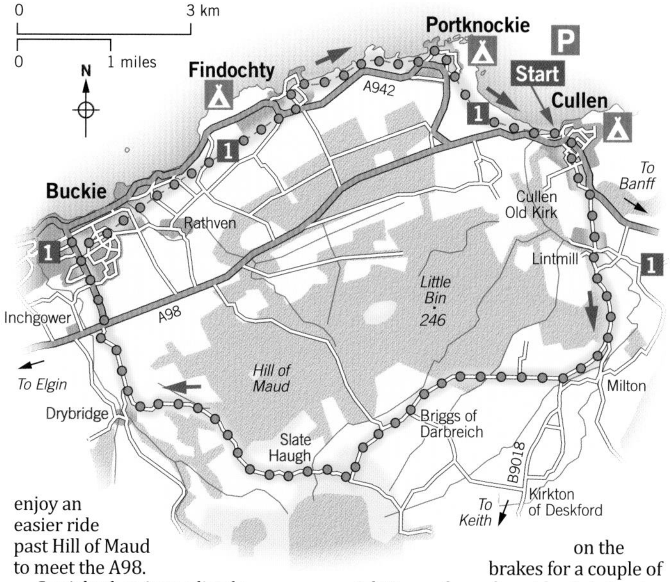

enjoy an easier ride past Hill of Maud to meet the A98.

Go right then immediately left to follow the A942 towards the coast at Buckie, going straight on at a roundabout. Further on, turn right immediately after the first church on your right to join NCN Route 1 again.

A cycle path cuts between a small supermarket and another shop to meet Wallace Avenue. Keep straight on at the roundabout onto Bruce Avenue then follow the cycle route sign towards Cullen beside the next roundabout.

From here you follow the scenic Route 1 east along the coast, initially following the line of the railway into Findochty. Go right on a cycle path alongside the main road then turn left to drop down into the village, keeping on the brakes for a couple of right turns through residential streets.

Above a glorious bay the route continues on a coastal path before rejoining the old railway line into Portknockie, where you can take a short walk to see the spectacular Bow Fiddle Rock. Find it by heading straight on down a road past some boat sheds where Route 1 goes right, away from the sea. The footpath to it is marked along the Moray Coast Trail to Cullen.

Continue on the cycle route to rejoin the former rail line above Cullen Bay and cycle over the viaduct.

Drop right at the end to immediately climb steeply up North Deskford Street. Turn left onto Grant Street to return to the square and explore the wonderful little village of Cullen.

CYCLE 6

Climb into lonely Glen Loth on a road ride with a difference

Grade 2 Very steep hills on rough road and one long busy trunk road section
Distance 27 miles / 44 km
Start/finish Helmsdale
Surface Busy trunk road, minor road with lots of ruts and bumps, single-track road; cattle grids
Map OS Landranger 17

The gold rush that brought hopeful prospectors to the Strath of Kildonan in 1869 is a far cry from the gentle pace of life the area now offers.

Cycling through lonely Glen Loth to reach the gold-carrying Suisgill and Kildonan burns is a joy, with hardly any traffic (it's a good job because there aren't really any passing places on the rough-and-ready road) and fine views once the col is reached.

This scenic triangular route involves six miles of riding on the busy A9 trunk road, something I wouldn't normally recommend – but unless you can arrange to be dropped off at Lothbeg and met in Helmsdale, it's a necessary evil.

Head south on the A9 from Helmsdale, passing through Portgower and continuing until you see the sign right to Glen Loth – don't be tempted to take the Lothmore turn a couple of miles north of there.

Select a low gear and carefully cross the A9 to take the Glen Loth road, which climbs very steeply past a sign warning that the road is not cleared in winter. Keep climbing high into the glen before a view to Beinn Dhorain, the highest of the Glen Loth hills, opens up and the gradient eases before dropping for a while.

Cross the stone bridge over the burn running down through Glen Sletdale, where one of the last wolves in Scotland is said to have been killed at the turn of the 18th

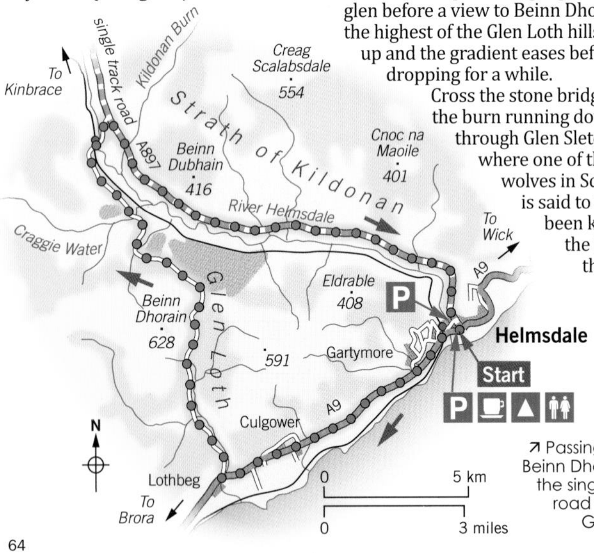

↗ Passing below Beinn Dhorain on the single-track road through Glen Loth

century, and pass two standing stones that mark the entrance to the glen.

From here the road, which is passable on a road bike but might be better ridden on a hybrid or mountain bike, slowly climbs below the bulk of Druim Dearg and Beinn Dhorain to reach a bealach on the east ridge of Ben Uarie just before a forest plantation.

It is here that a magnificent view comes into sight, with the distinctive peaks of Morven and Scaraben among a long line of Caithness hills visible over the trees.

The road descends steeply now and care is needed on this particularly bumpy and potentially fast downhill. Through gaps in the trees to your right you can get a first glimpse of the Strath of Kildonan before the road bends sharply right, over a small bridge, to pass a shed on the left then drops further to a bridge over the Craggie Water at a spectacular gorge.

Ride alongside the railway line now until a slightly unusual level crossing marked only with a "give way" sign. Cross carefully then go over the River Helmsdale, following the road past Kildonan Lodge to a T-junction. Turn right and follow the road down the strath to the Baile an Or, site of the short-lived gold rush.

You can still get a licence from the Suisgill Estate to have a go at gold panning in the burn for yourself.

The riding is all gently downhill now on this beautiful single-track road through the strath, which heads straight back into the heart of Helmsdale.

CYCLE 7

Cross-country mountain biking at its best on this welcoming Highland estate

Grade 2 Waymarked ride with some rough off-road sections and steep hills
Distance 11 miles / 18 km
Start/finish Campdalmore car park, A939 just north of Tomintoul
Surface Forest and estate tracks, some very rough; grass and heather paths; minor road; very hilly and extremely boggy in places; gates, stiles and steps; livestock may be present on some sections
Map Glenlivet Estate cycle trail leaflet from Tomintoul visitor centre or www.glenlivetestate.co.uk

Rough riding amid spectacular wild country make this waymarked cycle trail a challenging but rewarding outing. It's not the usual sort of bike route you'll find promoted – this one goes down steep, bumpy paths, across boggy moorland and through some remote places.

That's what makes it such a great ride for me. The distance isn't massive but that doesn't mean it's a quick and easy trip.

From the Campdalmore car park, follow the Scottish Rights of Way Society sign towards Dorback, initially on a good farm track with views left to the Cairngorms. Beyond the farm, go left on a grass track that bumps its way down to a house at Urlarmore. After a gate go right past the house to drop to the B9136.

The official route goes left then right onto the A939 to cross the Bridge of Avon – though it's possible to turn right to visit the old bridge and cross here, emerging at the road at the next turning.

From the road, go left to follow the right of way sign on a track, keeping right at the entrance to Kylnadrochit Lodge to climb into the forest. Further ahead, stay right at a house then fork left on the forest track, passing through a metal deer gate.

Where the forestry ends, turn right to climb steeply up a grass track (signed to Bridge of Brown) then continue to a gate on boggy ground. Go diagonally left across the moor and heather from here and follow the fairly obvious path above a ruined farmhouse at Tombreck.

The path disappears among fields but the very rough track – and I use the word cautiously; it's more like a rocky river than any kind of track – can be picked up to reach the forest, where a better track goes through a dark tunnel of trees.

It gets rough and boggy again beyond the trees until you are almost at the road by the Bridge of Brown, where the blue route markers point right up the remains of a steep grass path. It's barely bikeable but then the steep road is pretty tough too, so it's worth pushing the bike up here to miss out one of the hairpin bends on the road.

The path stops above a crash barrier and you need to cross carefully here – again, it's better to walk given the terrain – and turn right onto the main road.

Climb steeply through one S-bend to eventually reach the entrance to a forest on the left. Go through the gate and bear right a few hundred metres ahead to follow the main forest track which eventually starts to drop, offering a fast descent towards the minor road in Strathavon. After a turning circle a much rougher section drops even more steeply to reach the road after a stile.

Turn right onto the road and, at the bottom of the hill, look out for the suspension bridge across the river. Walk across this bouncy bridge and turn left in the field, turning right beside the first fence before the burn to climb to a gate that leads you onto the B-road.

Go left then right onto the minor road that climbs below Carn Meilich – past the new mountain bike centre – and continue ahead at a turn to Glenconglass to head through Croughly. At a sharp left-hand bend, go right through a gate into a field and carefully descend diagonally left (walking at least the last drop) to a bridge over the Conglass Water.

Climb the steps the other side and follow the Speyside Way marker left along the field boundary to pick up a soggy track that returns to Campdalmore.

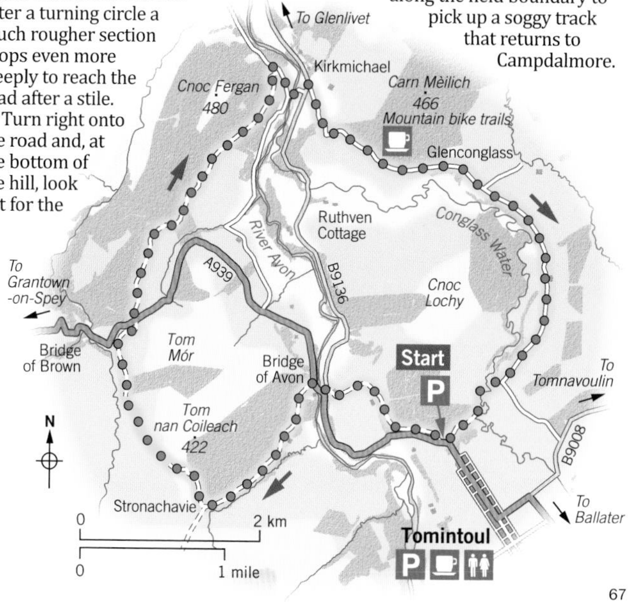

CYCLE 8

Off-road fun on a Cairngorms mountain bike adventure

Grade 2 Some rough riding and navigation required
Distance 18 miles / 29 km
Start/finish Glenmore Visitor Centre
Surface Forest and estate vehicle tracks, rough and bumpy in sections; minor and B roads; avoidable flood danger on private road
Map OS Explorer 403; Trailmap, Strathspey Map 5

You have to take the rough with the smooth on this exciting trip through two fantastic little passes. Most of the climbing – and there isn't too much of it for such a route – is on good surfaces, while in places it can be stony and boggy under your wheels.

In return you can expect impressive views, a wild experience and a true burst of adrenaline in one of the best areas in Scotland for outdoor activities.

Start out at the visitor centre car park – where there's a £2 charge for

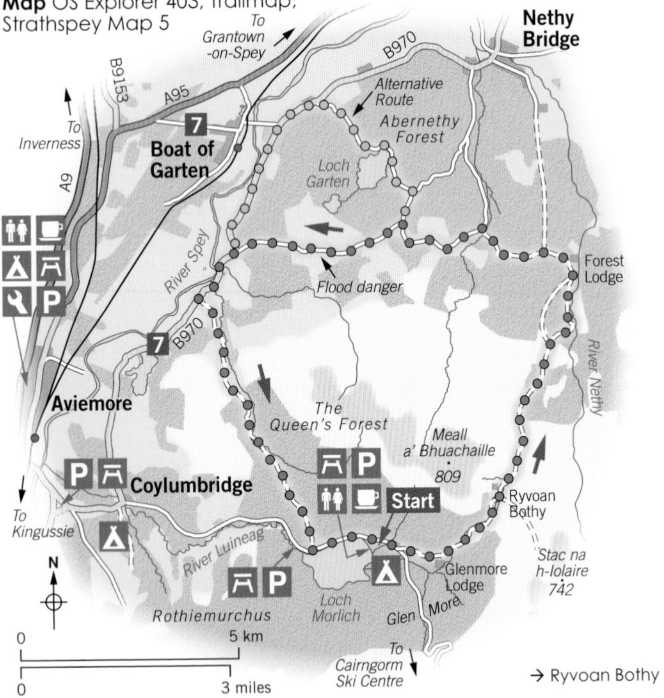

→ Ryvoan Bothy

parking – and follow the road beyond the youth hostel before turning left past the reindeer centre to Glenmore Lodge. Divert left onto the signed cycle and walkway and follow the right of way sign towards Forest Lodge and Nethy Bridge on an excellent track.

Pass a small lochan – An Lochan Uaine – before continuing on a rougher surface, keeping left at a fork, to Ryvoan Bothy, a shelter maintained by the Mountain Bothies Association.

Stay on the obvious track which continues across open moorland and through forest to Abernethy, ignoring a left turn which leads to Rynettin before keeping left where an older track continues to ford the River Nethy.

You soon arrive at an angled crossroads, going straight on to reach a gate with a good vehicle track beyond it. Go left onto this track and follow it to the public road below Tore Hill.

Turn left to follow the single-track road past a series of houses dotted here and there. The main route takes the first tarmac road left – still marked as a public road on older OS maps but now private. It's possible to cycle this way and emerge on the B970 but a large, deep and potentially dangerous flood often hinders progress.

An alternative route is to continue around the Tore Hill loop road and take the next left to pass Loch Garten and the RSPB osprey centre, coming out a few miles further up the B road.

Either way, turn left on the B970 and continue until you pass a white cottage at West Croftmore and a plantation beyond it. Immediately after the trees, go left onto a track opposite a National Cycle Network sign at a small white marker for Kincardine Cottage.

Pass a couple of houses and go through the right-hand gate to follow the An Slugan pass back to Glenmore. The track, muddy in places, climbs to a wooden gate then continues high above the Milton Burn before starting to drop through the forest.

Fork right where the track splits and watch out for give-way signs where the route crosses a vehicle track used to access the outdoor centre at Badaguish. Loch Morlich lies ahead – before the road go left onto the Old Logging Way, an off-road trail which leads back to the visitor centre.

CYCLE 9

Cycle from the station to reach the most northerly point on mainland Britain

Grade ❶ Main road sections but straightforward route with a few hills
Distance 32 miles / 51 km
Start/finish Thurso railway station
Surface Mostly minor roads with a few stretches on main road
Map OS Landranger 12

Lying just seven miles short of the nearest point on the Orkney Isles, Dunnet Head is the true northern tip of mainland Britain.

It might not get the recognition of John O'Groats at the north-east tip but a ride out to its lighthouse across the sometimes bleak moor makes for a fascinating outing.

The route starts at Thurso, where the nearest railway station is, and passes the Flagstone Trail at Castletown and the wonderful sandy beach of Dunnet Bay.

From the station go to the main road and turn right to head down it. Look out for the National Cycle Network signs directing you right, through the square then straight over at traffic lights to briefly join the A9 as it crosses the river.

↗ Milepost on way to lighthouse
→ A sign welcomes you to Dunnet Head

DUNNET HEAD
MOST NORTHERLY POINT OF MAINLAND BRITAIN
WELCOME

Go left at the next lights opposite the supermarket and then go right a few hundred metres up the road to climb between houses and away from the town.

As you get higher you can see Orkney on a clear day and even make out the Old Man of Hoy – the 137m (449ft) sea stack made famous by a BBC outside broadcast of a climb up it in 1967.

Further up the hill take a left turn to Castletown, following the magnificent single-track road down as it twists then drops to the village. Go straight on to cross the main road and follow a fine minor road past the start of the short Flagstone Trail walk and beyond the harbour which overlooks Dunnet Bay.

Turn left to follow the A836 briefly before heading right,

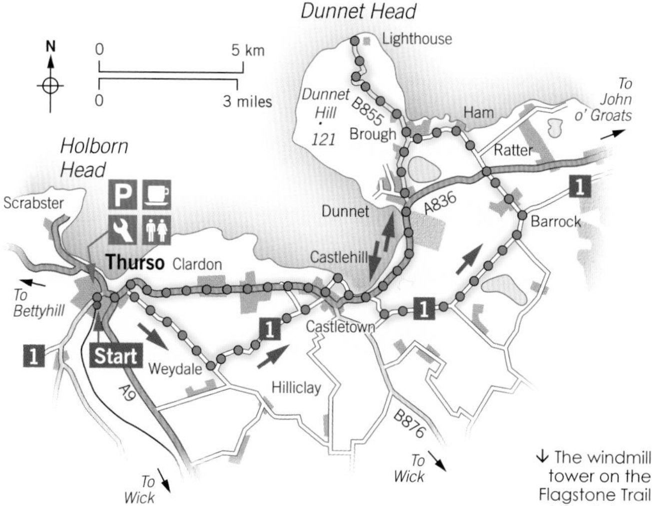

still following NCN Route 1. After some houses, go left at a T-junction then, a mile further on, take a left turn signed to Barrock.

Soon you leave the cycle route, going left to follow the "Barrock ¼" sign and continue to the A836 again. Follow the sign for Dunnet Head straight on, taking the fabulous road to Ham which hugs the shore as it passes a ruined watermill beside a lochan.

The road continues to Brough, where a right turn takes you on the out-and-back road to the end of the headland.

Milestones count down the three miles to the lighthouse from here as the road passes through an exposed land of lochs and hillocks, steering up a wide hairpin to the highest point until eventually the road runs out at a car park beside the lighthouse.

Reminders of World War II are all around in the form of lookouts on the hill, which also has a viewpoint if you take the short walk or ride to the top.

On the return journey, take a right turn at Brough towards Thurso to pass St John's Loch and return to the main road. Go right here and follow it around the glorious Dunnet Bay and back through Castletown to Thurso.

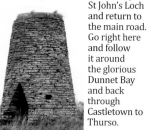

↓ The windmill tower on the Flagstone Trail at Castletown

CYCLE 10

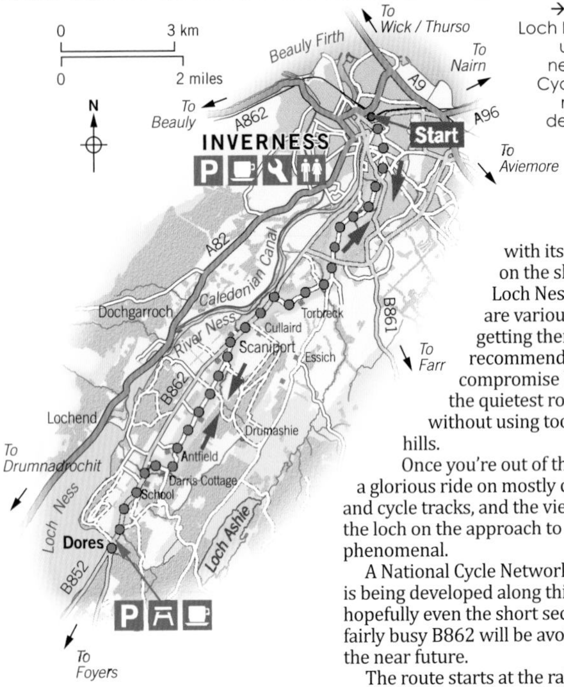

→ The ride to Loch Ness makes up part of a new National Cycle Network route under development

Visit Loch Ness on this quiet ride from the heart of Inverness

Grade 1 Mostly quiet roads
Distance 19 miles / 30 km return
Start/finish Inverness railway station
Surface Minor road and cycle path
Map OS Landranger 26; Inverness cycle map

One of the most popular rides for visitors to Inverness is a trip to Dores, with its long beach on the shore of Loch Ness. There are various ways of getting there but my recommendation is a compromise between the quietest roads without using too many hills.

Once you're out of the city it's a glorious ride on mostly quiet roads and cycle tracks, and the view over the loch on the approach to Dores in phenomenal.

A National Cycle Network route is being developed along this way so hopefully even the short section on the fairly busy B862 will be avoidable in the near future.

The route starts at the railway station, from where you exit to Falcon Square (the exit to your right as you face the trains) and head for the pedestrian crossing across the paved area to your right. Go straight up Inglis Street and turn left on the main pedestrian precinct at Eastgate.

Before reaching the road, veer right up the steep Stephen's Brae then continue effectively straight on at the double junction at the top to join Kingsmills Road, with the church then school on your left. Fork right at the traffic lights to join Southside Road and

continue to the next lights beside the Crown Court Hotel. Go left here then immediately right. As the road bends left, turn right again onto Muirfield Road and follow it to a T-junction, where you turn right.

Head straight over at the traffic lights, now entering Drummond Road, and dip over a burn before following the long, straight road for around 1km until it turns sharply right after a school. Turn left onto the tree-lined Lochardil Road then go left again at the traffic lights to follow Stratherrick Road.

You are now almost out of the city as you go straight over the Essich roundabout, taking a right turn onto a minor road to Torbreck after the housing estate. This stretch of road is great as it flows down through crofts and woodland to reach the main road.

Turn left and stay on the B862 for just over 1km until Scaniport, where you can turn left to join another beautifully quiet single-track road. The views down the Great Glen start to become visible now but it's a little further until you can see the waters of Loch Ness.

At a junction, turn right then look out for a new cycle track on the left just after the houses at Darris. This links up with an older shared-use path after the school at Aldourie which you can follow all the way into Dores if you prefer to stay off the main road.

As you drop down the hill you get the best view of the loch, with the prominent hill of Meall Fuar-mhonaidh rising above its north-west shore. It's lovely on a summer's evening or early in the morning when the light can make the view even better.

At Dores there's a pub serving food, walks around Tor Point, a children's play park, a Nessie hunter's caravan and, of course, the beach to enjoy.

CYCLE 11

A fine Highland circuit taking in castles, distilleries and mountain views

Grade 1 Easy country roads with one or two hills
Distance 21 miles / 34 km
Start/finish Tomintoul
Surface Minor roads and quiet B roads
Map OS Landranger 36

Take a trip to the highest village in the Highlands where you'll find quiet roads waiting to be explored by bike. This wonderful circuit explores Strath Avon before passing a castle once occupied by the notorious Wolf of Badenoch and a famous whisky distillery.

You'll get views of the Cairngorms and head below Carn Diamh, the highest point on the Speyside Way and a walk described in this book.

From the main car park in the centre of the village (free parking) go left and follow the A939 in the direction of Grantown-on-Spey. Soon you drop to cross the River Avon and climb the other side, still on the main road.

Take a right turn onto a minor road

in a dip and you'll pass a peculiar stand-alone stone chimney beside the road.

This "lum" was used by roadside workers in the 1920s and '30s to erect a small wooden shelter against where they could light a fire to keep warm.

This fabulous quiet road follows the river downstream, crossing the Burn of Lochy before cruising below the Cromdale Hills then heading on a bridge over the Avon to meet the B9136. Turn left towards Glenlivet.

After meandering along this road you catch sight of Drumin Castle, a 14th-century castle thought to have been built after King Robert II gifted these lands to his son, Alexander Stewart – the Wolf of Badenoch.

To reach the castle, go past the farm at a right-hand bend then turn sharp left down a hill to reach a car park, from where there's a short walk to explore the castle.

Continue over the bridge on the minor road and up the hill to meet the B9008. Turn right then, after another 1km, turn right just before a cemetery before going left 100 yards further on towards the Glenlivet Distillery.

The road leads through the whisky plant and up into the hills beyond. Turn left at a T-junction and enjoy fine views over the distillery and surrounding countryside, including the prominent Ben Rinnes.

After Gallowhill there's a lovely descent for a couple of kilometres as the road descends to Tomnavoulin to meet the B road again. Go right through the village and up a long hill to pass Auchnarrow until the ascent finally comes to an end.

You're almost back at Tomintoul now as you descend to cross a narrow bridge over the Conglass Water and go straight on past a junction for Braemar via the Lecht.

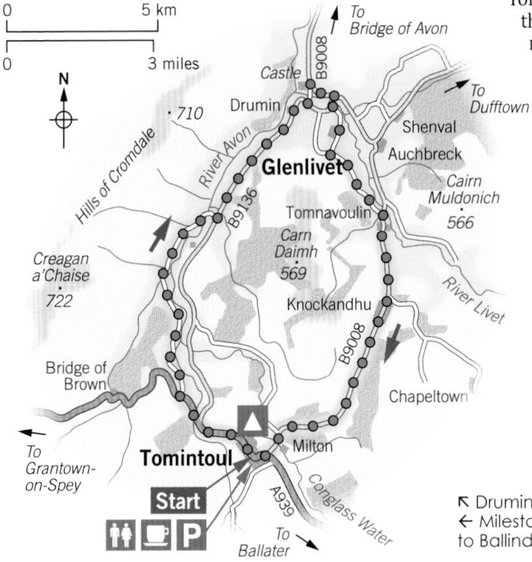

↖ Drumin Castle
← Milestone on road to Ballindalloch

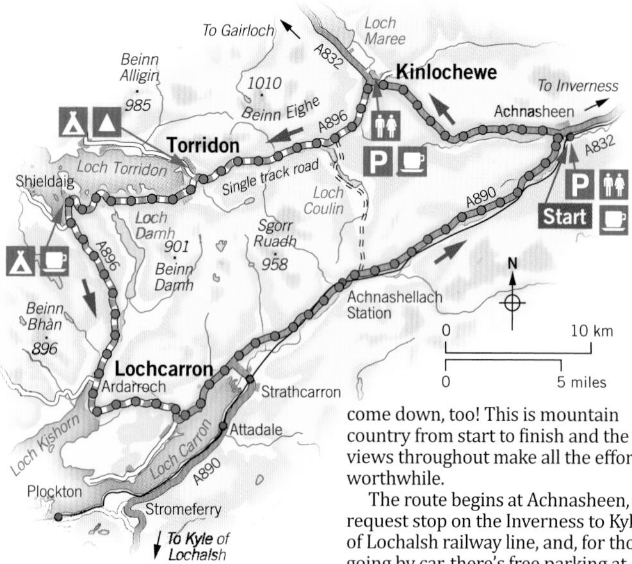

↙ Riding in Glen Torridon towards Liathach

Cycle through Glen Torridon below its dramatic peaks on this grand ride around Wester Ross

Grade 3 Long hilly ride
Distance 63 miles / 101 km
Start/finish Achnasheen station
Surface Single carriageway and single-track A roads; cattle grids
Map OS Landranger 24 & 25

This classic tour of Wester Ross is a glorious ride, passing through Glen Torridon before visiting Shieldaig and Lochcarron on some beautiful single-track and single-carriageway roads.

It has its fair share of hills to climb – but what goes up must come down, too! This is mountain country from start to finish and the views throughout make all the effort worthwhile.

The route begins at Achnasheen, a request stop on the Inverness to Kyle of Lochalsh railway line, and, for those going by car, there's free parking at the station opposite the public toilets, signed from the A832.

Cycle west through the village to join the main road and follow it left to a roundabout 100 yards ahead. Turn right here for Kinlochewe and Gairloch and you're away on this epic ride.

A gentle start sees you follow the pretty Loch a' Chroisg before climbing to a popular viewpoint above Kinlochewe. Down Glen Docherty you can see Loch Maree beyond the village and the impressive Munro of Slioch rising above its north shore.

Better still, it's the start of four miles of downhill that mean your brakes will need a good test! After crossing a large cattle grid, enter Kinlochewe and turn left onto the single-track A896 signed to Torridon. The next 10 miles is a real highlight, spinning through this famous glen with Beinn Eighe and Liathach dominating the skyline.

At Torridon, follow the road to the left around the head of Upper Loch Torridon through Annat and then up a fairly strenuous climb which opens up a magnificent view of Beinn Alligin, the third of the large Torridon peaks, across the loch.

Beyond the viewpoint drop down again to Shieldaig. Don't miss this wonderful little place, which is easy to do if you just stay on the main road.

Turn right at the village sign and follow the minor road past the campsite and down to the shore. Continue through the village and veer right to rejoin the A896, heading inland through Glen Shieldaig past Loch Dughaill.

Another pass climbs to 130 metres here before heading back down to sea level at the turn-off for the Bealach na Ba road to Applecross. Yet another climb – though not as strenuous as that route – awaits between here and Lochcarron before you head steeply down to the bustling loch-side village.

Railway stations at Strathcarron and Achnashellach offer an escape from the last of the hilly sections but for those intent of completing the circuit there's still some effort to put in over the last 20 miles or so.

Go straight on after leaving the village to join the A890 through a nice woodland stretch before crossing the river at Coulags on a nice stone bridge. After crossing the railway and going through Achnashellach, you'll climb to Craig before even more uphill leads you high into Glen Carron.

By the time the ascent eases, it's only a few more miles on a wide open road to the roundabout at Achnasheen, the first junction for 18 miles!

CYCLE 13

Link this end-to-end adventure with public transport for a great day out

Grade 3 Remote but all on tracks and roads, some rough
Distance 30 miles / 48 km
Start/finish Black Bridge (A835 north-west of Garve) / Ardgay
Surface Tarmac and stony estate tracks; short sections very rough, most easily rideable
Map OS Landranger 20; OS Explorer 437

There's nothing quite like cycling through Highland glens surrounded by hills and lochs, and this route allows you to enjoy the experience without any technical mountain-biking skills.

With a few miles of tarmac at each end and the rest mostly made up of easily rideable rocky tracks, this is a route that's achievable by any reasonably fit rider. I can't guarantee there won't be a few seriously boggy sections and concentration will certainly be required, but satisfaction is definitely on the cards.

Even better, this linear route is well linked (at least in summer) by public transport from Inverness – by taking the Highland Bike Bus to the start at the Black Bridge and returning by train from Ardgay. With a bit of planning it makes a fine day out in the remote glens of Ross-shire and Sutherland.

From the Black Bridge, take the private road up Strath Vaich, soon heading through a gate into a farmed area where cows and sheep stroll alongside the open track.

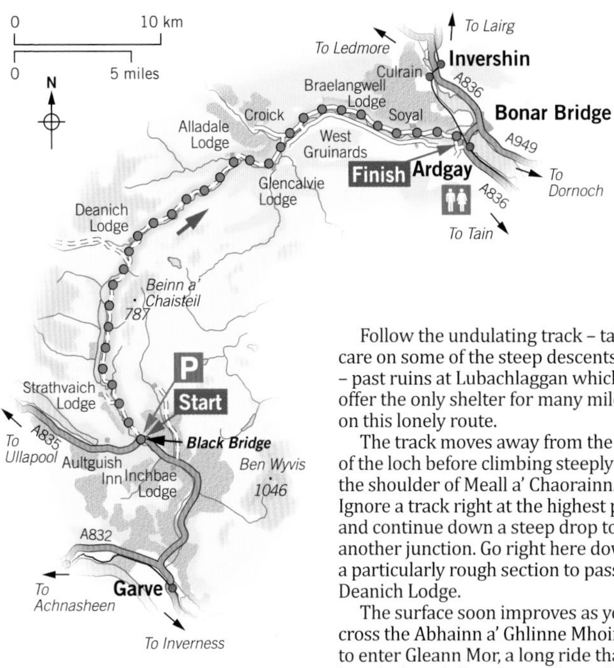

↖ Crossing the bridge into Gleann Mor

At a weir, keep straight ahead to join a rough track where the tarmac continues left towards the lodge. Follow the edge of a forest plantation then, after crossing a bridge, keep left to climb to a rise high above Loch Vaich, the views opening up as you reach the summit.

Follow the undulating track – taking care on some of the steep descents – past ruins at Lubachlaggan which offer the only shelter for many miles on this lonely route.

The track moves away from the end of the loch before climbing steeply over the shoulder of Meall a' Chaorainn. Ignore a track right at the highest point and continue down a steep drop to another junction. Go right here down a particularly rough section to pass Deanich Lodge.

The surface soon improves as you cross the Abhainn a' Ghlinne Mhoir to enter Gleann Mor, a long ride that's largely downhill or flat until you drop steeply to cross a bridge over the Alladale River. After a second bridge (over a tributary) turn right and follow this beautiful stretch to the public road at Glencalvie Lodge.

Continue ahead on the tarmac, turning right at a T-junction a few kilometres further on. After a mile, turn right to cross the River Carron to follow the minor road on the south side of the river back to Ardgay.

➲ For details of the Highland Bike Bus, see Cycle 2: Ullapool to Lochinver. Check train times and ticket prices at www.scotrail.com

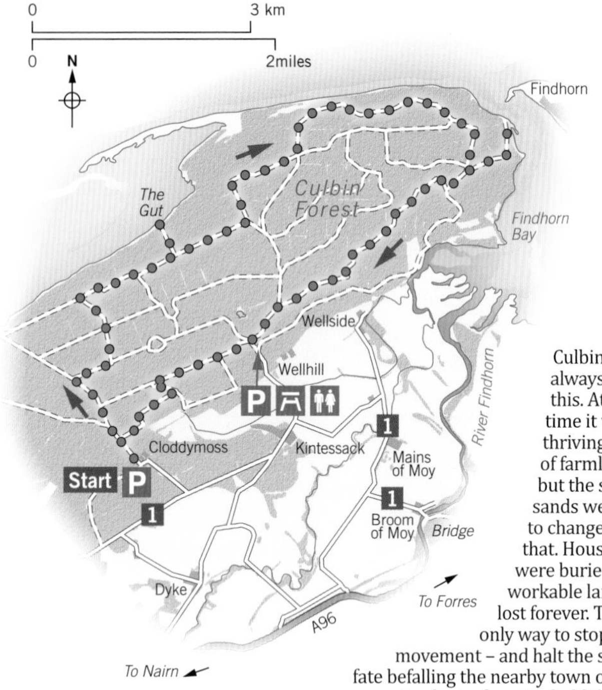

→ Across Findhorn Bay from Culbin

Reach Findhorn Bay on this pedal through a unique forest

Grade 1 Traffic-free cycling on excellent forest tracks
Distance 13 miles / 21 km
Start/finish Cloddymoss car park, Culbin Forest
Surface Forest tracks throughout – can be muddy at times
Map Culbin Forest leaflet (Forestry Commission)

Culbin wasn't always like this. At one time it was a thriving area of farmland but the shifting sands were to change all that. Houses were buried and workable land was lost forever. The only way to stop the movement – and halt the same fate befalling the nearby town of Nairn – was to plant a forest to hold the sand in place.

Now Culbin Forest, managed by the Forestry Commission, is teeming with wildlife and is a popular place for walkers, runners, horse riders and cyclists. With so many tracks through this woodland, which stretches along 14km of the coast, the junctions have all been numbered and a detailed leaflet makes navigation simple.

This ride starts out at the Cloddymoss car park – where a £2 charge applies – and heads down to

the shore before approaching the beautiful Findhorn Bay.

Head down the track and fork right at Junction 34, going straight on at J35 and turning right at a rare unmarked junction in the middle of an area of younger trees. At the next junction (J38) visit the "Hidden History" which explains what happened to the houses and land here in the 17th century.

Go left here and right at J15 to head for The Gut, an area of salt, sand and shingle which teems with wading birds. Stay left at J14 then go left to detour to The Gut on the shoreline, which is managed by the RSPB as a nature reserve. Continuing on the main track again, take a left at J13 and stay left at J8 to Buckie Loch where the sea crashes over the golden dunes at high tide.

To get to Findhorn Bay, keep left at J5 then turn left at a sign at J3. Follow the track round and it's possible to access the beach overlooking the complex mouth of the River Findhorn, with the village visible on the far side.

Back at J3 head for "Lady Culbin's Trees", going right down the hill at J4. The trees are unusual here as they taper towards the bottom, rather like the tip of a pencil, because the dunes covered their bases while they were younger. The trunk above the sand continues to grow while that below the sand remains thinner.

Continue to J2, bearing left towards the busy Wellhill car park, then go straight on through the next couple of junctions. At J37, go left onto the grassy track then right at J36 to skirt by the edge of a field before reaching J33 near the start. Turn left to head back to Cloddymoss.

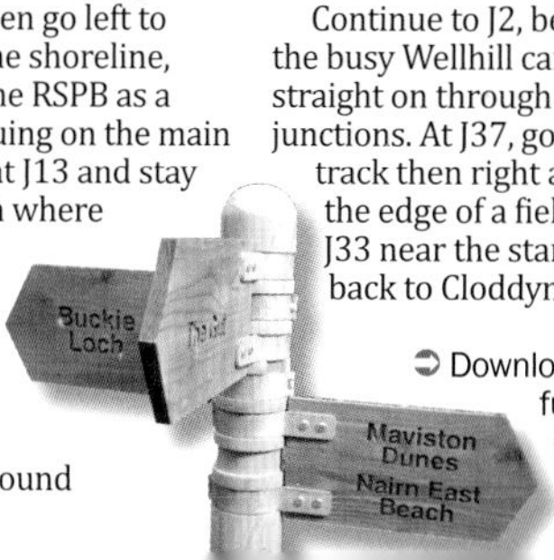

➲ Download the map and get further information on the forest at www.culbin.org.uk

CYCLE 15

A scenic tour in south-east Sutherland

Grade ❷ Short stretches on trunk road
Distance 30 miles / 48 km
Start/finish Dornoch
Surface Mostly quiet minor roads but two sections on busy A9
Map OS Landranger 21

Visiting a remote loch, this road circuit makes use of some of the quieter highways and byways around this part of the Highlands. In places you're unlikely to see much traffic at all, though to complete the loop requires making use of the A9 in a couple of short bursts.

Starting in the centre of Dornoch, follow the main road out towards the A9 and turn left onto Sutherland Road, which heads out of the town on a

minor road past Lonemore and Cuthill, going right to pass over a nice stone bridge before it meets the main road.

Carefully turn right onto the A9, which is wide here so not too daunting for traffic-confident cyclists. You follow the road for about a mile then go left onto the A949 towards Lairg and Bonar Bridge.

At Ospisdale pass the Clach a'Charra Standing Stone, which local tradition suggests marks the grave of a Danish chief, before climbing gently up to Spinningdale. Drop down through the S-bends and slow down as you look

The Clach a'Charra Standing Stone beside the A949
↗ Passing through woodland near Migdale

out for a hidden right turn signed to Migdale.

This enticing single-track road takes you up through forest and out to the open hillside with fantastic views ahead. Ignore a left turn to Migdale and continue instead to a crossroads.

Take a right here to head to the lonely Loch Buidhe, climbing to the high point of the route at 188m before getting your first view of the loch. The road is not treated in winter beyond the house at Sleastary.

What follows is a delightful ride that descends gently along the edge of the water then down the picturesque "Srath Carnaig", the narrow tarmac running parallel to the tumbling river that heads down to River Fleet and our own destination, Loch Fleet.

Towards the bottom a dramatic waterfall can be seen from the roadside. Continue as the road flattens and meets the A9 at The Mound, where you go carefully right to follow the trunk road for 1km then cut left onto a minor road to Embo and Dornoch.

This is one of my favourite roads to cycle because it closely follows the shore of the stunning Loch Fleet with all sorts of wildlife to spot, including seals and wading birds.

Take your time to enjoy this gentle stretch before the road bends right to pass the turn-off to Embo and continue downhill into the centre of Dornoch.

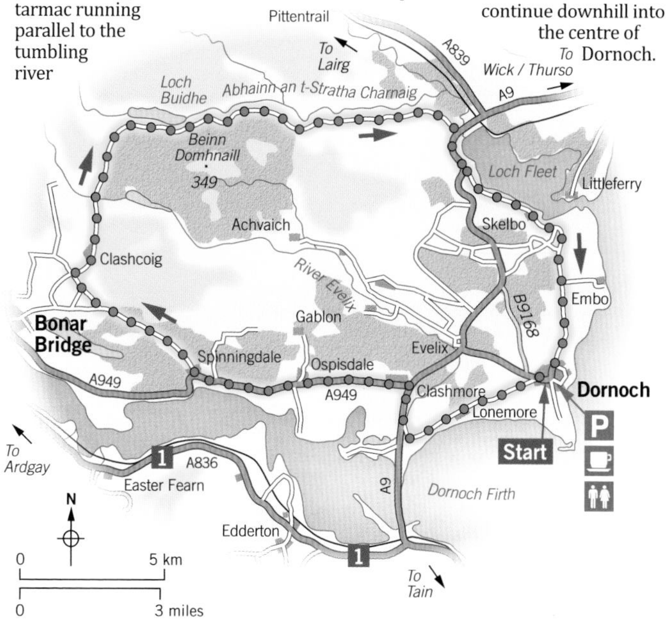

CYCLE 16

A great day in the saddle as you explore Cairngorms villages

Grade 3 Rough sections and some map-reading required
Distance 33 miles / 53 km
Start/finish Aviemore
Surface Minor roads, cycle paths, farm and forest tracks – rough in places
Map OS Landranger 36

A combination of on and off-road cycle routes makes this triple loop an exciting outing with some challenging cycling. You'll need to take a mountain bike to enjoy the rougher sections – and enjoy them you will!

This area is a real highlight of the National Cycle Network but, although the route should be largely signed, a map is essential to follow the various twists and turns – as there isn't room here to describe every one in detail.

Starting in Aviemore, pick up NCN Route 7 (off-road) towards Boat of Garten, heading through the Dalfaber estate before joining the Speyside Way beside a golf course. A beautiful section runs parallel to the Strathspey Railway then, beyond a gate, goes left under the rails and right along a track to Boat of Garten.

Go left at a T-junction and follow the road then a tarmac cycle path on your left as you exit the village until you meet the A95. Follow the path to the crossing point (right of the road junction) and take a track opposite which soon climbs to Docharn farm, where the route swings sharp left and continues into the forest.

The route to Carrbridge is fairly obvious now, sticking to the main track to emerge finally at a gate. Go through the gate and ahead to the road, turning left into the village.

With two of the three off-road sections now complete, our route switches to the road option to reach Slochd at the northernmost point. Turn right at the junction in Carrbridge then follow the main road past the ruinous packhorse bridge and round the left-hand bend to climb through woodland.

← The Strathspey Railway passes over the off-road section between Aviemore and Boat of Garten

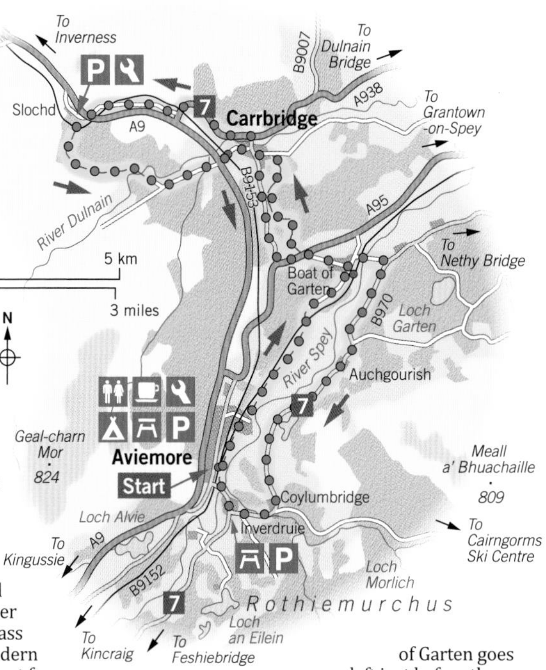

After going under the railway and just before reaching the A9, turn right towards Slochd on a minor road that makes for wonderful cycling. Further along you'll pass under the modern A9 then look out for a sharp left turn after a hostel, which takes you onto the final off-road section – back to Carrbridge.

This is a great downhill section, needing care in places, that goes past Incharn then left towards the eye-catching Sluggan Bridge. Continue beyond the bridge, taking a left fork to reach a minor road. Turn left to return to Carrbridge.

Next to the old packhorse bridge again, turn right onto the B9153 and follow the road this time to its junction with the A95. The cycle route to Boat of Garten goes left just before the junction to another crossing point, the cycle route continuing on the far side to join up with the one you followed out of Boat of Garten earlier.

This time continue through the village, following the road left then right and over the River Spey to a T-junction. Go right here and follow the long B970 all the way to Coylumbridge.

Turn right to return to Aviemore, picking up the excellent traffic-free Old Logging Way on the far side of the road for a fine end to this inspirational Cairngorms adventure.

CYCLE 17

A remote off-road circuit from a quiet railway station

Grade ❷ Signposted tracks
Distance 16 miles / 26 km
Start/finish Altnabreac railway station
Surface Estate tracks, rough in places
Map OS Landranger 11

Step off the train at Altnabreac and you enter a very different world.

On the single platform there's a small notice board that shows a map of the tracks in this area, including this 16-mile circuit passing Loch More and the ruined Dalnawillan Lodge.

It's a remote ride that doesn't pass any public roads – unless you use the alternative start which you can approach by road from Westerdale past Strathmore Lodge – yet it's all marked on mostly reasonable estate tracks.

This route starts at the railway station and follows the waymarked red route – though many of the discreet arrows have faded to white.

Exiting the station, turn left onto the main track which runs parallel to the railway line running north-east. The surface is smooth (between the potholes) and easy to ride on a hybrid or mountain bike, and it continues like this for most of the route.

Follow the track right to Loch Caise, where a boggy footpath can lead you closer to the water's edge if you dismount. Back on route, hug the shore through a nice S-bend before going deeper into the forest past Garbh Loch then out to an opening which overlooks Loch Gaineimh.

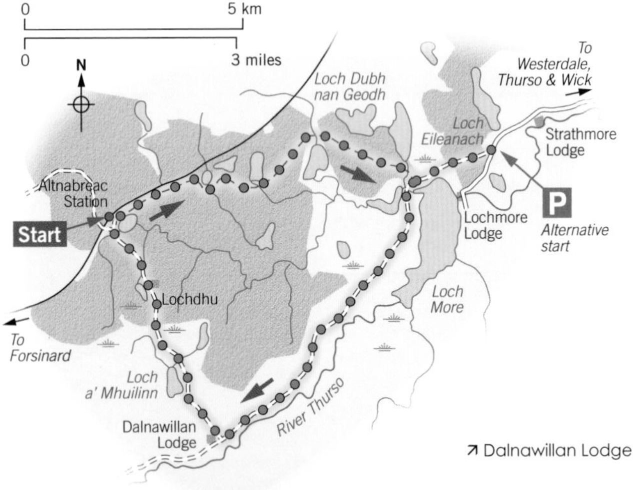

↗ Dalnawillan Lodge

After the next stretch of forestry, you come to a gate and a junction. Over the low gate, turn right and go over another gate across an inviting causeway and bridge. Here you are crossing the Sleach Water (on your right) as it enters Loch More (to the left).

Follow this enticing track the length of the loch then past a track junction before continuing towards Dalnawillan Lodge. It's flat all the way along here and makes for easy cycling – so long as it's not windy!

Just before the lodge the dogs of Dalnawillan will no doubt give you a rousing reception from within their kennels. It's often a noisy experience passing here but you then arrive at the ruined and somewhat eerie Dalnawillan Lodge.

A wooden signpost outside directs you right, pointing four miles back to Altnabreac. This track is bumpier to begin with and it rises slightly to reach the beautiful Loch a' Mhuilinn.

From there, head into the forestry again and pass the rather unusual and extravagant Lochdhu Lodge – once a hotel but now a private residence – on the shore of the loch of the same name.

Drop downhill then keep right at a fork to cross the Sleach Water again, heading right at the next signpost to return to the station.

Altnabreac is a request stop, so you'll need to check the train times and allow enough time for your ride. It'll be worth the effort as the train takes you home after this fantastic outing.

CYCLE 18

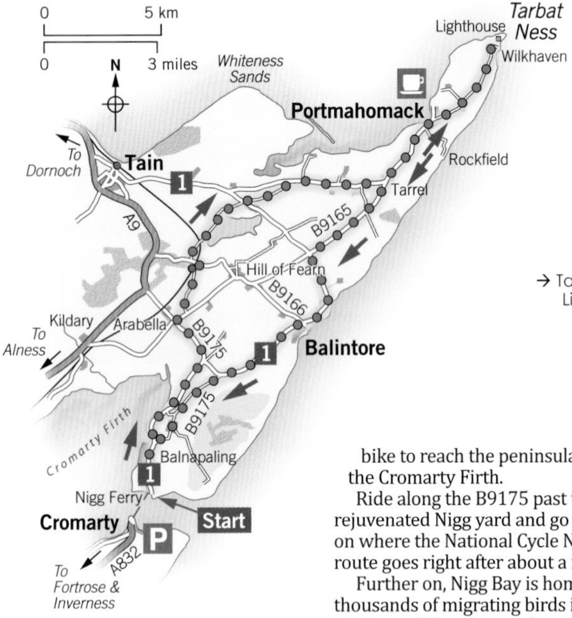

→ Tarbat Ness Lighthouse

Take the ferry for a seaboard ride to a classic lighthouse

Grade 2 Largely flat road ride
Distance 37 miles / 60 km
Start/finish Nigg Ferry (Cromarty)
Surface Minor single-track and B roads
Map OS Landranger 21; OS Explorer 438

The red-and-white striped lighthouse at Tarbat Ness is the target of this largely flat cycle that begins at Nigg Ferry – or rather at Cromarty, where you can hop on the ferry with your bike to reach the peninsula across the Cromarty Firth.

Ride along the B9175 past the rejuvenated Nigg yard and go straight on where the National Cycle Network route goes right after about a mile.

Further on, Nigg Bay is home to thousands of migrating birds in the winter and there's a modern RSPB hide a short walk from the parking area. Continue to Arabella, where you turn right towards Hill of Fearn, then, shortly after a residential street, go left off a long straight to join a narrow road that leads to the station at Fearn – an alternative start point for this ride, especially if the ferry is out of action.

Go left over the railway then right towards Loandhu to pass Loch Eye on a wonderful single-track road, going through an unmarked crossroads to a T-junction with views across the firth to the north-east coast.

Turn right and soon there's a small climb to the junction with the B9165,

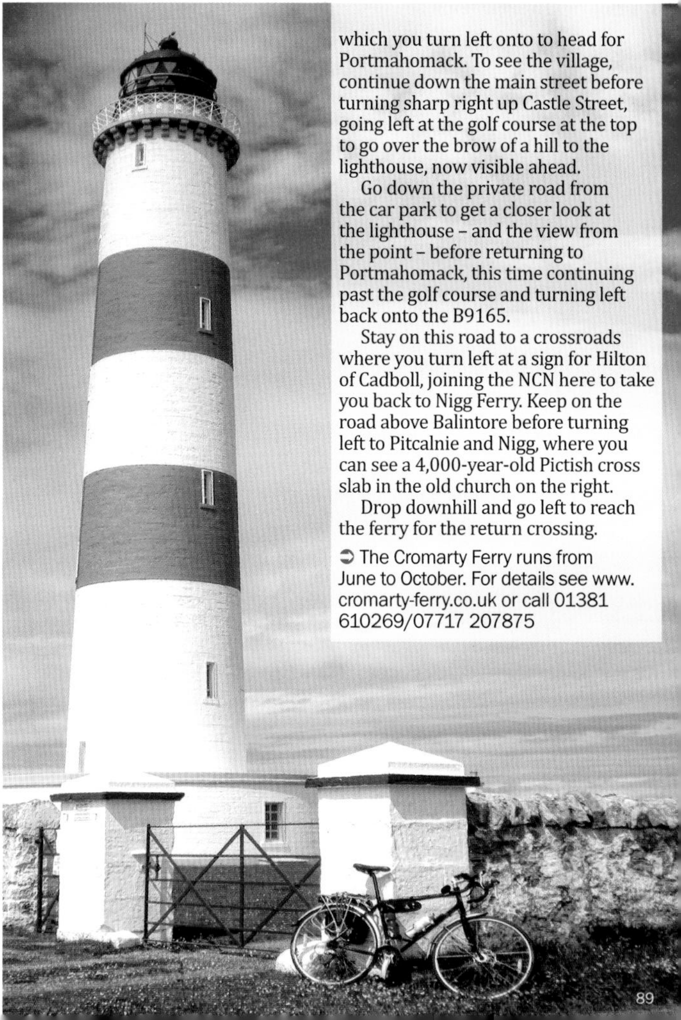

which you turn left onto to head for Portmahomack. To see the village, continue down the main street before turning sharp right up Castle Street, going left at the golf course at the top to go over the brow of a hill to the lighthouse, now visible ahead.

Go down the private road from the car park to get a closer look at the lighthouse – and the view from the point – before returning to Portmahomack, this time continuing past the golf course and turning left back onto the B9165.

Stay on this road to a crossroads where you turn left at a sign for Hilton of Cadboll, joining the NCN here to take you back to Nigg Ferry. Keep on the road above Balintore before turning left to Pitcalnie and Nigg, where you can see a 4,000-year-old Pictish cross slab in the old church on the right.

Drop downhill and go left to reach the ferry for the return crossing.

➲ The Cromarty Ferry runs from June to October. For details see www.cromarty-ferry.co.uk or call 01381 610269/07717 207875

CYCLE 19

Climb where eagles soar on a trip to the Black Isle

Grade 2 Some hills and main roads to cross
Distance 24 miles / 38 km
Start/finish Dingwall
Surface Minor roads and tarmac cycle track
Map OS Landranger 26

Mount Eagle is the highest point on the Black Isle, the lovely peninsula between the Moray and Cromarty firths, at 256m above sea level. This route starts in Dingwall, the old county town of Ross-shire, and rises to a short distance below the masts that adorn its summit.

It's a fabulous road that links Culbokie on the northern edge of the peninsula and Munlochy at the south.

To reach it, turn left out of the railway station in Dingwall, following National Cycle Network signs left towards Inverness at the traffic lights. A shared-use path leads along the A862 to the roundabout before Maryburgh, where you turn left to cross the River Conon at its mouth.

At the first junction the cycle route swings left then joins a minor road right that runs parallel to the A835 as it climbs through beautiful countryside past Torgorm.

Turn left at the T-junction to leave the cycle route and follow the B9169 through Easter Kinkell and continue until you reach the A9, with views over the Cromarty Firth and Ben Wyvis much of the way. Going right then left, carefully cross the A9 to head towards Culbokie, still on the B road.

The route to Mount Eagle begins the far side of the village, turning right immediately after the playing fields on a minor road towards Munlochy. There's a 100m climb to the forest crossroads at the top of the hill, from where you can access a number of tracks that offer walks in the woods, including taking you the short distance to the summit.

Continuing down the road past the Belmaduthy Dam Reserve, a fine descent can be enjoyed with glorious views to the south – but look out for a staggered junction as it starts to level. Turn right and follow the twisting road through the farm before continuing along this beautiful quiet road to a crossroads. Go straight on towards Tore and continue until the next junction, where you turn left shortly after a large farm at Mains of Tore and just the other side of a burn.

Follow the bumpy road then turn right onto the A832. Just before the roundabout, cross to the right to join a cycle track which crosses the A9 exit then turns right through an opening in a wooden fence. At the corner of a short residential road, a path drops left to run alongside the A835. This is a fine community link path to connect Dingwall and Inverness and now makes up part of the NCN.

Follow it past forest walks at Monadh Mor then enjoy the view over Ben Wyvis ahead as it starts to descend. Where the path swings right, follow the B road right then go left to rejoin the route back to Dingwall.

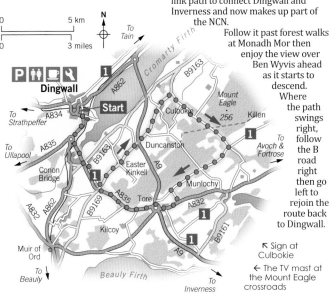

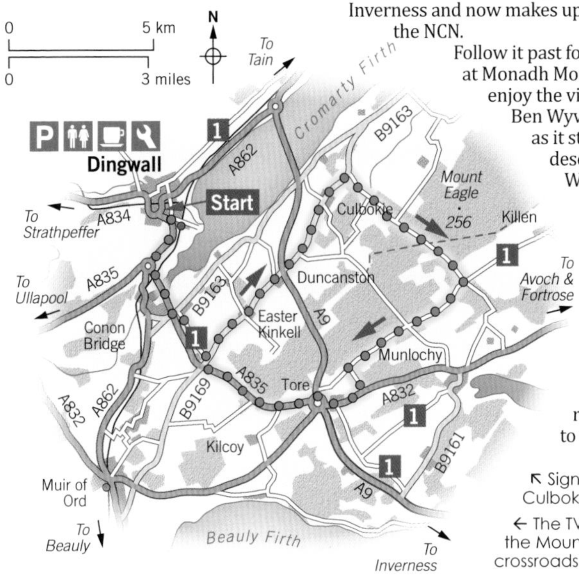

↖ Sign at Culbokie

← The TV mast at the Mount Eagle crossroads

CYCLE 20

Go west to the cape to reach the north-west tip of mainland Britain

Grade ❷ Straightforward directions but hilly and remote
Distance 22 miles / 36 km return plus detours 3 miles / 5 km
Start/finish Keoldale, near Durness (Cape Wrath Ferry)
Surface Badly eroded tarmac road – mountain bike required; rough, steep track to bothy on detour
Map OS Landranger 9

Access to Cape Wrath

The ferry runs seven days a week from May to September. Follow signs to Cape Wrath Ferry off the A838 just south of Durness. For more information visit www.capewrathferry.co.uk or call 01971 511246.

To check MoD activity, check with ferry operator or call the MoD info line on 0800 833300 or 01971 511242.

There is a peculiar fascination with Cape Wrath – its sheer inaccesibility makes it a place to seek out. The north-west tip of mainland Great Britain lies about 12 miles from the nearest road across rough and desolate moor, much of which is owned by the Ministry of Defence and can be closed if live firing is taking place.

Yet it's far from impossible to access this remarkable corner of the country. You could walk from the south, a good path leading to Sandwood Bay before around eight or nine miles of pathless trudging northwards.

There's even a minibus in the summer that takes tourists out to the lighthouse – but for me it's much better to get there by bike.

The Cape Wrath Ferry carries passengers over the Kyle of Durness during the summer to meet the minibus, which travels along the 11-mile track to the cape.

You can take your bike over on the ferry and tackle the rough track yourself. The only traffic you'll meet is the minibuses that go backwards and forwards – though with a lack of passing places you might need to hop out of the saddle to allow them to pass!

As a very rough guide, it takes around an hour-and-a-half each way for a reasonably fit cyclist, but don't

Kearvaig bothy

→ Mile marker on road to lighthouse

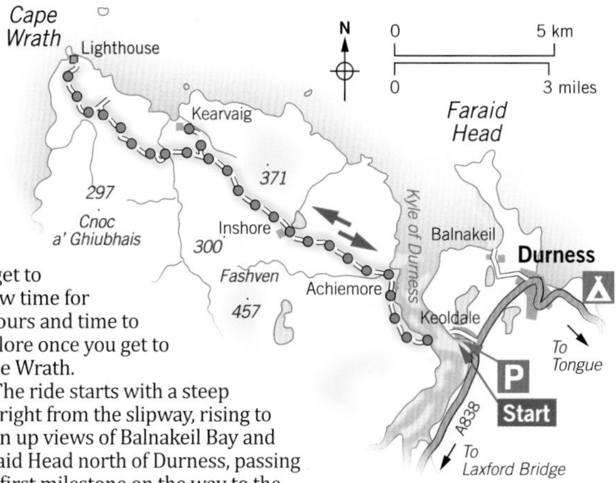

forget to allow time for detours and time to explore once you get to Cape Wrath.

The ride starts with a steep hill right from the slipway, rising to open up views of Balnakeil Bay and Faraid Head north of Durness, passing the first milestone on the way to the lighthouse.

After the initial climb, the old road levels out to contour around the hill before dropping to the start of the MoD land. You won't miss it – there are plenty of warning signs and if the red flags are flying it means there's live firing happening. If not, carry on to cross a bridge at Daill, a beautiful little inlet, then climb again to the high point of the ride 5km hence, with a little bit of respite between two lochans and views of Fashven off to your left.

Pass a cairn that marks a detour down to Kearvaig bothy then cross an old humped-back bridge at some more MoD buildings. The track continues up and round to the right to pass a building before swooping down to an unusual thing – a junction! Turn left and climb again round the shoulder of Dunan Mor, behind which lies Cape Wrath lighthouse. At last you get your first glimpse of this end-point of the ride.

Surprisingly there's a café in this rather remote spot – not only that but the Ozone Café is open 24 hours a day, all year. It serves a great cup of tea and has some interesting information about the history of the lighthouse on the walls, as well as selling a small selection of souvenirs.

On the way back it's possible to detour to a jetty near the junction, though there's little to see there. However, the detour to the bothy is definitley recomended, despite the very steep and rough track down to the bay. It might involve a slow walk back up the hill but the bay is stunning and the bothy superbly kept.

The return ride is slightly easier than the outward route but there are still some uphill stretches to tackle. Make sure you check with the ferryman on return times or you could have a long wait!

CHECKLIST

Walk 1 ❑ Date................Notes

Walk 2 ❑ Date................Notes

Walk 3 ❑ Date................Notes

Walk 4 ❑ Date................Notes

Walk 5 ❑ Date................Notes

Walk 6 ❑ Date................Notes

Walk 7 ❑ Date................Notes

Walk 8 ❑ Date................Notes

Walk 9 ❑ Date................Notes

Walk 10 ❑ Date................Notes

Walk 11 ❑ Date................Notes

Walk 12 ❑ Date................Notes

Walk 13 ❑ Date................Notes

Walk 14 ❑ Date................Notes

Walk 15 ❑ Date................Notes

Walk 16 ❑ Date................Notes

Walk 17 ❑ Date................Notes

Walk 18 ❑ Date................Notes

Walk 19 ❑ Date................Notes

Walk 20 ❑ Date................Notes

Cycle 1 ❑ Date................ Notes

Cycle 2 ❑ Date................ Notes

Cycle 3 ❑ Date................ Notes

Cycle 4 ❑ Date................ Notes

Cycle 5 ❑ Date................ Notes

Cycle 6 ❑ Date................ Notes

Cycle 7 ❑ Date................ Notes

Cycle 8 ❑ Date................ Notes

Cycle 9 ❑ Date................ Notes

Cycle 10 ❑ Date................ Notes

Cycle 11 ❑ Date................ Notes

Cycle 12 ❑ Date................ Notes

Cycle 13 ❑ Date................ Notes

Cycle 14 ❑ Date................ Notes

Cycle 15 ❑ Date................ Notes

Cycle 16 ❑ Date................ Notes

Cycle 17 ❑ Date................ Notes

Cycle 18 ❑ Date................ Notes

Cycle 19 ❑ Date................ Notes

Cycle 20 ❑ Date................ Notes

Read John's blog at BL6.co.uk or follow him on Twitter @BL6John and Facebook at facebook.com/BL6John

Acknowledgements

After the unexpected success of my first book, *John Davidson's Guide to Walking and Cycling in Inverness and the Highlands*, I decided to put together a second collection of routes covering an even wider area.

This was only possible thanks to massive support from my family, particularly my wife Meg and my two young daughters, Clara and Jennifer – who have enjoyed one or two of the easier trips in this book with me!

I'm also hugely grateful to my big brother Iain, who designed the cover as well as continuing to encourage me through our shared love of the outdoors.

I'd like to thank Helen Stirling for producing the excellent maps in this guide; Peter Evans for joining me on many of the routes; Alan Hendry for his proof-reading skills; Philip Waite (Highland Council access officer for Ross-shire) for assistance and advice; and all the readers of Active Outdoors – I hope this guide lives up to your expectations!

All the best,
John

↓ On the top of Sluggan Bridge on the Aviemore-Slochd ride (Cycle 16)